You Are What
You Think

ALSO BY DR. WAYNE W. DYER

BOOKS

Being in Balance
Change Your Thoughts—Change Your Life
Co-creating at Its Best (with Esther Hicks)
Don't Die with Your Music Still in You (with Serena Dyer)
The Essential Wayne Dyer Collection (comprising *The Power of Intention,*
Inspiration, and *Excuses Begone!* in a single volume)
Everyday Wisdom
Everyday Wisdom for Success
Excuses Begone!
Getting in the Gap (book-with-audio-download)
Good-bye, Bumps! (children's book with Saje Dyer)
I Am (children's book with Kristina Tracy)
I Can See Clearly Now
Incredible You! (children's book with Kristina Tracy)
Inspiration
The Invisible Force
It's Not What You've Got! (children's book with Kristina Tracy)
Living the Wisdom of the Tao
Memories of Heaven
My Greatest Teacher (with Lynn Lauber)
No Excuses! (children's book with Kristina Tracy)
The Power of Intention
The Power of Intention gift edition
A Promise Is a Promise
The Shift
Staying on the Path
10 Secrets for Success and Inner Peace
Unstoppable Me! (children's book with Kristina Tracy)
Your Ultimate Calling
Wishes Fulfilled

You Are What You Think

365 Meditations for Extraordinary Living

DR. WAYNE W. DYER

HAY HOUSE, INC.
Carlsbad, California • New York City
London • Sydney • New Delhi

Published in the United States by: Hay House, Inc.: www.hayhouse.com®
· **Published in Australia by:** Hay House Australia Pty. Ltd.: www.hayhouse.com
.au · **Published in the United Kingdom by:** Hay House UK, Ltd.: www.hayhouse
.co.uk · **Published in India by:** Hay House Publishers India: www.hayhouse.
co.in

Quotes selected and edited by Ned Leavitt with invaluable support from Shannon Littrell and Nicolette Salamanca Young.

Cover design: Scott Breidenthal · *Interior design:* Nick C. Welch

**Cataloging-in-Publication Data is on file with
the Library of Congress**

Tradepaper ISBN: 978-1-4019-5603-5
E-book ISBN: 978-1-4019-5604-2

10 9 8 7 6 5 4 3 2 1
1st edition, October 2018

Printed and bound in Great Britain by
TJ Books Limited, Padstow, Cornwall

I came home from school one day, and I asked
my mother, "What is a scurvy elephant?"
She said, "I don't know. I don't know
what a scurvy elephant is. Why?"
I said, "Well, I heard the teacher saying that
Wayne Dyer was a scurvy elephant
in the classroom."
She got right on the phone and talked to
the teacher, and the teacher said, "No, I didn't say
that at all. I said Wayne was a disturbing
element in the classroom."
I've always been that scurvy elephant.

INTRODUCTION

Do you remember the first time you encountered the words of Dr. Wayne W. Dyer? Many of us have fond remembrances of watching one of his PBS specials or seeing him speak onstage at one of the events he so loved doing throughout the years. Perhaps you were browsing the shelves at a bookstore and found yourself drawn to a title, only to discover words that would change the course of the rest of your life. Whichever way we discovered him, so many lives were touched by his charismatic yet grounded way of speaking and writing.

If this is your first encounter with the wisdom of Wayne, however, you may be wondering who this man is and what this book has in store for you! One of Hay House's most beloved authors, known worldwide as "the father of motivation," Wayne was at the forefront of the personal transformation movement for decades. He was endlessly curious about new ideas and new approaches to psychology and spirituality, always excited to plunge deep into a new adventure then come out sharing what he had discovered. He was a unique speaker, writer, and personality whose insights reached millions over the span of his long and productive career.

The story of how Wayne began as an author is legendary—ordinary publishing channels didn't have a mechanism for promoting him back in 1976 when he wrote his first book, *Your Erroneous Zones*, teaching people to transcend errors in their thinking. So Wayne bought books from his publisher, put them in the trunk of his car, and hit the road, seeking out small radio and TV stations that would give him a chance to share his groundbreaking message. And audiences responded— switchboards lit up with viewers and listeners asking where they could get his books. His big break came when he landed a regular spot on *The Tonight Show Starring Johnny Carson*. With this nationwide platform for sharing his message, it wasn't long before he started appearing on other popular shows of the time, including *The Phil Donahue Show*, the *Today* show, *The Merv Griffin Show*, and *Good Morning America*. *Your Erroneous Zones* became the number-one-selling nonfiction book of the decade, eventually being published in 47 languages around the globe, with total sales of around 100 million copies worldwide. Other highly successful psychological books soon followed.

After a time, Wayne started moving away from traditional psychology as the foundation of his message. A meeting with Viktor Frankl inspired him to commit to teaching and living from a place of meaning. He began following the promptings of new spiritual insights, feeling a call to write about personal and spiritual transformation. He was drawn to the works of the great philosophers and Eastern and Western spiritual wisdom, from the Bhagavad Gita and the Tao Te Ching to the New Testament. Brushing aside the skepticism of his publisher and agent at the time, he confidently followed his dharma. His new books were warmly received by audiences, debuting on the *New York Times* bestsellers list.

Throughout his career, Wayne had a number of editors and publishers who supported his evolving message in different ways. When he finally landed at Hay House in the '90s, however, he found a spiritual home and supportive environment for the rest of his days. During the two decades of his relationship with Hay House, he continued to grow and refine his spiritual message, publishing multiple *New York Times* bestsellers, including *10 Secrets for Success and Inner Peace, The Power of Intention, Inspiration, Change Your Thoughts—Change Your Life, Excuses Begone!, Wishes Fulfilled,* and *I Can See Clearly Now,* which were all featured as National Public Television specials.

Wayne never shied away from connecting with his fans, and his generosity and support for helping others find their voice was legendary. He met so many inspirational people through serendipitous ways, and when he found himself struck by someone, he *had* to know their story—and help them share it with the world. Some accompanied him to speak and perform at various events, such as Dan Caro, the inspirational young man who became a jazz drummer even after a fire robbed him of the use of his hands. Some went on to become published authors, including Anita Moorjani and Immaculée Ilibagiza, who are both now *New York Times* best-selling authors and internationally renowned motivational speakers.

◆◆

In this tribute book of quotes, we at Hay House are proud to offer a sampling of Wayne's inspiring insights together in one place. Wayne made a lifelong practice of expressing his ideas, achieving the kind of mastery of self-expression that comes only with true dedication. It may be surprising to find such a range of articulation—sometimes the unwinding of a complex thought, sometimes the perfect aphoristic bon mot. How did Wayne's writing strike so many different and intriguing notes? We believe that when writing is a daily practice, the self-conscious plans of the ego are subsumed by the mind and spirit tuning in to larger voices and larger streams of thought—some arising from consciousness and some from uncharted realms. And, like Wayne, we all have many different voices floating inside us. No matter what voices we hear—old parental voices, loving voices from our partners, encouraging voices from our therapist, warning voices from those that oppose us in some way, or unexpected guidance from unknown sources—all are opportunities for insight or growth.

This book can be used in many ways. In sequential order, you might use it as a daily encounter with one of Wayne's many voices. Each day's offering may or may not feel in sync with what your day may bring, but will definitely stimulate you. You can consider the quote either as something to be in tune with or something to argue with. You can also look for guidance on specific dates that have meaning for you, such as birthdays, wedding days, memorial days for beloveds, or days when something important is to take place. Or you can use the book as a random oracle: open to any page and see what synchronicity brings to your attention. Are the words you find a perfect fit for what you were seeking? Or is it more contrary or enigmatic, an offering that requires looking deeper into your mind, heart or spirit? Listen to the voice of Source within. As Wayne always used to say, "We talk to God when we pray, and when our intuition speaks, that is God answering."

JANUARY 1

Commit yourself to your own magnificence. Every time you look into a mirror, remind yourself that what stares back at you is not an ever-changing body, but an invisibleness that is truly your highest self. Affirm: *I am love, I am God, I am worthy, I am infinite,* silently and out loud. Do this frequently so that it eventually becomes your inner mantra. This will help you abandon old patterns you've carried that have injured your personal relationship to this universe and all of the inherent beauty and perfection it holds. You will awaken to the incredible miracle that you are.

JANUARY 2

We are all Divine creations and should always treasure the fact that we carry God around with us wherever we go. We emanated from the spirit, and the spirit is nothing more than pure love. The flesh—that is, our bodies—is not who we truly are. Who we really are is a piece of what we came from, and that is Divine love.

JANUARY 3

Ever seen that bumper-sticker slogan "This is the first day of the rest of your life"? Well, I prefer thinking that this is the *last* day of my life—and I'm going to live it as if I didn't have any more. Because the truth is that we don't know. The past is over for all of us. The future is promised to none of us. All we get is now—the present—and if you don't know that you're going to have to face a last day, you haven't really been alive. Death is as important a part of life as living it.

JANUARY 4

Keep reminding yourself: *I get what I think about, whether I want it or not.*

JANUARY 5

Abundance is what God's kingdom is about. Imagine God thinking, *I can't produce any more oxygen today; I'm just too tired. This universe is big enough already; I think I'll erect that wall and bring this expansion thing to a halt.* Impossible!

❖

JANUARY 6

Forgiveness is an act of self-love.

JANUARY 7

Loving sacredly means loving what is, even if you don't comprehend the deeper meaning behind it.

JANUARY 8

Being creative means trusting your own purpose and having an attitude of unbending intent in your daily thoughts and activities. Staying creative means giving form to your personal intentions. A way to start giving them form is to literally put them in writing. For instance, in my writing space here on Maui, I've written out my intentions, and here are a few of them that stare at me each day as I write:

- *My intention is for all of my activities to be directed by Spirit.*

- *My intention is to love and radiate my love to my writing and any who might read these words.*

- *My intention is to do all that I can to elevate the collective consciousness to be more closely in rapport with the Spirit of the originating supreme power of intention.*

JANUARY 9

Detachment is the absence of a need to hold on to anyone or anything. It's a way of thinking and being that gives us the freedom to flow with life. Detachment is the only vehicle available to take you from *striving* to *arriving*.

JANUARY 10

Where I separate myself from most psychologists is, I have a strong belief that anyone can reach the highest levels of their humanity if they make the kinds of choices they have the capacity for making. All of us can operate at high, creative, no-limit levels. Many psychologists and therapists have written that there are a few chosen people, and those few are very special, unique. I don't think it's true. I think fulfillment and high levels of functioning are there for all of us.

JANUARY 11

Do what you want, as long as you're not interfering with anyone else's right to do the same—this is the definition of morality.

JANUARY 12

I've watched all eight of my children blossom into their own awakenings. They all showed up here at birth with their own unique personalities, perhaps from a series of previous lives—the mysterious possibilities are endless. But I know for certain that the one Divine mind that is responsible for all of creation has a hand in this engaging mystery. Same parents, same environment, same culture, and yet eight unique individuals, all of whom arrived with their own distinct character traits. I think Khalil Gibran stated it perfectly in *The Prophet*: "Your children are not your children. They are the sons and daughters of Life's longing for itself. They come through you but not from you, and though they are with you yet they belong not to you."

JANUARY 13

Has it ever occurred to you that beauty depends on something being identified as ugly? Therefore, the idea of beauty produces the idea of ugliness, and vice versa. Just think of how many concepts in this "duality belief system" depend on opposites: A person isn't tall unless there's a belief system that includes short. Our idea of life couldn't exist without that of death. Day is the opposite of night. Male is the antithesis of female.

What if you instead perceived all as a piece (or a glimpse) of the perfection of oneness? Surely the daffodil doesn't think that the daisy is prettier or uglier than it is, and the eagle and the mouse have no sense of the opposites we call life and death. The trees, flowers, and animals know not of ugliness or beauty; they simply *are* . . . in harmony with the eternal Tao, devoid of judgment.

❖

JANUARY 14

You'll be trapped emotionally and physically until you learn to forgive.

❖

JANUARY 15

The ones who are going to be part of the problem are the ones who believe that the problem is what makes them upset, therefore they can't do anything about it: *The problem has to go away before my upset-edness goes away.*

The people who are part of the solution are going to say: *This is the condition of the world, these are the things that are, and I am going to process them in such a way that I can change it.* These people can't be immobilized by their thoughts about things.

❖

JANUARY 16

How could we have ever owned anything at all?
The best that we can do is to have temporary possession of our toys for a tiny speck of time.

JANUARY 17

As a 10-year-old boy, I was introduced to two ideas that were guideposts for the journey that was to become my destiny. The first is that people will respond for the benefit of all concerned if you speak to them with confidence and in a nonjudgmental manner. The second guidepost is that there's a secret garden where miracles and magic abound, and it's available to anyone who makes the choice to visit there.

❖

JANUARY 18

I have often told my children that before I incarnated into this lifetime, I had a conversation with God, in which I told Him/Her that all I wanted to do for this entire journey was to be a teacher of self-reliance. And God responded by saying, "If that is your true intention, then we better get you into an orphanage for a decade or so, where you will come to know self-reliance firsthand, and then no one will ever be able to dissuade you that such a thing is not always possible."

JANUARY 19

Pay attention to times when you can feel in your body where you are on the continuum between trying and doing. *Trying* to play the piano, drive the car, or ride the bicycle is the same as, and different from, actually playing the piano, driving the car, and riding the bicycle. Once those outer-world activities are desired and learned, there's a time when allowing is what you do. The point here is to recognize the difference in your body between trying and allowing, and to then become aware of the effortless sensation of the latter. This practice will also lead to a greater awareness of the invisible mystery and the 10,000 things, which are the visible phenomena of our world.

JANUARY 20

When you're kind to others, you receive kindness in return. A boss who's unkind gets very little cooperation from his employees. Being unkind with children makes them want to get even rather than help you out. Kindness given is kindness returned. If you wish to connect to intention and become someone who achieves all of your objectives in life, you're going to need the assistance of a multitude of folks. By practicing extending kindness everywhere, you'll find support showing up in ways that you could never have predicted.

JANUARY 21

Let the world unfold without always attempting to figure it all out. Let relationships just be, for example, since everything is going to stretch out in Divine order. Don't try so hard to make something work—simply allow. Don't always toil at trying to understand your mate, your children, your parents, your boss, or anyone else, because the Tao is working at all times. When expectations are shattered, practice allowing that to be the way it is. Relax, let go, allow, and recognize that some of your desires are about how you think your world *should* be, rather than how it *is* in that moment. Become an astute observer . . . judge less and listen more. Take time to open your mind to the fascinating mystery and uncertainty that we all experience.

JANUARY 22

When you squeeze an orange, you get orange juice because that's what's inside. The very same principle is true about you. When someone squeezes you—puts pressure on you—what comes out is what's inside. And if you don't like what's inside, you can change it by changing your thoughts.

JANUARY 23

There's nothing to worry about—*ever*! Either you have control or you don't. If you do, take control; if you don't, dismiss it. Don't waste your energy on worry.

JANUARY 24

Your body is nothing more than the garage where you temporarily park your soul.

JANUARY 25

Tell me what you're *for*, and I'll show you what's going to expand in a positive way. Tell me what you're *against*, and I'll show you what's going to expand in a destructive way.

JANUARY 26

The greatest service that can be offered to children who show personality traits or inclinations that might not be understood by the adults around them is to allow them to express their own unique humanity. I was blessed to be able to live much of the first decade of my life in an environment where parental and other adult meddling in my life was kept to a minimum. I know that I came into the world with what I call "big dharma"—with a blueprint to teach self-reliance and a positive loving approach to large numbers of people all over the globe. I am ever so grateful for the circumstances of my life that allowed me to be pretty much left alone and to develop as I was so intended in this incarnation.

JANUARY 27

Each one of us is part of a perfect universe. And we are as much a part of the universe as anyone else or anything else that's in it. In a perfect universe, which works on harmony and cooperation and love, there are no mistakes. So *you* are not a mistake. You are a part of the perfection of it. If you believe that about yourself, the first time you begin to see other people behaving abusively toward this perfection, this object of beauty and this object of importance, then you react the way you naturally would react to someone who's abusing something beautiful: You wouldn't allow it.

JANUARY 28

The essence of greatness is the ability to choose personal fulfillment in circumstances where others choose madness.

❖

JANUARY 29

Most people who are lonely are lonely because they don't like the person they're alone with. If you like the person you're alone with, being alone is never a problem. It's just terrific. But if this person I'm alone with is really sort of contemptible and unacceptable to me, then I'm looking for somebody or something else to fill in the voids.

❖

JANUARY 30

All you get is today, and next week maybe. But today, for sure.

JANUARY 31

What I call "no-limit living," or "mastery," is going to the top of the ladder—that's where you become the same way a sculptor or painter or creator of any kind is to their creations. Shading, shaping, and making it into what you want it to be.

FEBRUARY 1

It's easy to love some people. The true test is to love someone who's hard to love. Send all your enemies love.

FEBRUARY 2

If you only believe what you see, then you're limited to what's on the surface. If you only believe what you see, why do you pay your electric bill?

FEBRUARY 3

You get treated in life the way you teach people to treat you. If you allow yourself to get pushed around, if you allow others to victimize you, if you allow people to beat you down, then you are teaching people how to treat you.

FEBRUARY 4

If the world were organized so that everything had to be fair, no living creature could survive for a day. The birds would be forbidden to eat worms, and everyone's self-interest would have to be served.

FEBRUARY 5

If you have a container that's full of manure, there's no room in the container for love or for anything else. We all have manure in our lives, but it's knowing what to do with the manure that's really important. If you take the manure and put it into the ground and use it for fertilizer, you can grow beautiful flowers with it.

FEBRUARY 6

It's a simple procedure to calculate the number of seeds in an apple. But who among us can ever say how many apples are in a seed?

FEBRUARY 7

If you can't say no within a relationship, you'll have to say no to the relationship eventually. *No*, the *n* word, is a big word to be able to say. By saying no in the relationship, you are letting other people know, including the people who love you the most—your parents, your children, your husband or wife, your affiliates, your business associates, your friends—that you have to be your own person. When they want you to be something that you can't be because it conflicts with where you are on your own path of enlightenment, of fulfillment, you have to say no to that. Ultimately, that will strengthen the relationship. You can say no with love and dignity and respect—and with commitment. Then you'll never have to say no to the relationship, because it will flourish and grow.

FEBRUARY 8

Many people have had a close brush with death; have had somebody close to them experience that; or maybe have been in an accident, where they have been there, on that bed, wondering whether they were going to survive. And people who have that kind of an experience almost always say, "It taught me the most valuable lesson of my life: that I've got to take each day that I live and make it complete, whole, fulfilling, creative, and exciting for me."

I believe it shouldn't have to take a brush with death to do something so natural, so simple, so basic, as to live your life the way you want to, on your terms, without having to answer to anyone else.

FEBRUARY 9

As individuals begin to align with their original intent and live a life on purpose, they invite in their highest guidance. I have come to know that the only way to access the assistance of the ascended masters is to become like them so that they can recognize themselves. It does no good to pray for guidance and help if we're living an ego-centered life.

FEBRUARY 10

I have a suit in my closet with the pocket cut out. It's a reminder to me that I won't be taking anything with me. The last suit I wear won't need any pockets.

FEBRUARY 11

So many people are expecting a miracle instead of *being* a miracle.

FEBRUARY 12

Everything you're against can be restated in a way that puts you in support of something. Instead of being against war, be *for* peace. Instead of being against poverty, be *for* prosperity. Instead of joining a war on drugs, be *for* purity in our youth.

FEBRUARY 13

All depression is inertia. That's where it comes from.

People would come to me and say, "I'm so depressed; I just don't know what to do."

I'd say to them, "Anything. *Anything.* You see that bicycle there: let's go for a ride. You see that ball over there: let's play catch with it. You see that hospital over there: let's walk through the corridors and talk to the people who are sick. Let's do *anything* . . ."

Because it's almost impossible to be depressed and active at the same time. Active people don't have time to get depressed. They're too busy.

FEBRUARY 14

If I'm to be a being of love living from my highest self, that means that love is all I have inside of me and all that I have to give away. If someone I love chooses to be something other than what my ego would prefer, I must send them the ingredients of my highest self, which is God, and God is love.

FEBRUARY 15

Blame is a neat little device you can use whenever you don't want to take responsibility for something in your life. Use it, and you'll avoid all risks and impede your own growth.

FEBRUARY 16

Your expectations determine so much about your life. They determine, for example, how physically healthy you are—whether you have colds, backaches, headaches, cramps, and things like that. You set yourself up to be sick, instead of saying: *This is a mistake. I'm not interested in this. I don't want this. I'm going to take a few extra pills of vitamin C, I'm going to get myself a little extra rest, but I'm not going to complain to anybody else about it. I'll see if I can go through this whole thing without letting it affect me. I'm also going to keep myself active. I'm not going to let it get in the way of anything that I'm doing. I'm not going to focus on it, and I'm not going to concentrate on it.*

FEBRUARY 17

Three things clog your soul: *negativity*, *judgment*, and *imbalance*.

FEBRUARY 18

You can't give away what you don't have. If you don't have love for yourself, then you can't be loving to others—so self-love is the name of the game.

FEBRUARY 19

Let's say you want to quit smoking—you want to eliminate addictive behavior in your life, whatever it may be. The only way that it's sensible to attack a problem like quitting smoking is to say to yourself, "Today, just today, can I go 24 hours—one day—or even a half a day, or even a few hours, without a cigarette?"

Well, I answer, "Of course. Anybody can go a day. That's no big deal."

At the end of that 24-hour period, you're a new person. Let that person decide whether they want to go another day. Because you're a new person every day. You just deal with your life one day at a time.

FEBRUARY 20

At some point today, notice an instance of annoyance or irritation you have with another person or situation. Permit the paradox of wanting the irritant to vanish and allowing it to be what it is. Look inward for it in your thoughts and allow yourself to feel it wherever it is and however it moves in your body.

Notice how the feeling manifests itself: perhaps doing loop-the-loops in your stomach, giving a rigidity to your skeleton, making your heart pound, or tightening your throat. Wherever it is, allow it as an enigmatic messenger within you, and give it nonjudgmental attention. Notice the desire for the feeling to disappear, and allow it to be monitored compassionately by you. Accept whatever comes. Encounter the mystery within without labeling, explaining, or defending. It's a subtle distinction at first, which you must take personal responsibility for identifying. You alone can prepare the ground of your being for the experience of living the mystery.

FEBRUARY 21

I don't believe that God is concerned with whether or not we show our love by building magnificent edifices for worship, by attending services, or through practicing rules laid down by religious organizations. It seems to me that if God were to speak to us, the message would simply be to love each other and offer reverence rather than enmity.

FEBRUARY 22

The elevator to success is out of order today. You're going to have to take the stairway, one step at a time.

FEBRUARY 23

To write about nonbeing as the place we originate *from* requires me to imaginatively speculate on what the spiritual world of nonbeing is. The way I do this is to imagine a Divine consciousness who's in the business of manifesting form out of nothingness. Imagining a creation without a Creator is a lot like trying to imagine a watch without a watchmaker.

FEBRUARY 24

You can't expect to draw people into your life who are kind, confident, and generous if you're thinking and acting in cruel, weak, and selfish ways. You must put forth what you want to attract.

FEBRUARY 25

Everything in the universe flows. You can't get hold of water by clutching it. Let your hand relax, though, and then you can experience it.

FEBRUARY 26

There is one grand lie—that we are limited. The only limits we have are the limits we *believe.*

FEBRUARY 27

I've found that every spiritual advance I've made was preceded by some sort of a fall—in fact, it's almost a universal law that a fall of some kind precedes a major shift. A fall can be an embarrassing event that reveals the exaggerated influence ego has been allowed to play in one's life, which certainly happened to me when I was prompted to end my association with alcohol. Other kinds of falls may involve an accident, a fire that destroys all the stuff we've worked so hard to accumulate, an illness, a failed relationship, a death or injury that causes deep sorrow, an abandonment, a serious addiction, a business failure, a bankruptcy, or the like. These low points actually provide the energy needed to make a shift in direction away from an ego-driven life to one full of purpose.

FEBRUARY 28

You see, everything in the universe comes in paradox, because we are in paradox because the planet is in paradox. Think about it. The paradox that you are is that you are form and nonform at the same time. You are your body, and yet you're not your body. You are your thoughts, which you can't get hold of, and yet you're your body, which has hold of you. And so you always have these two conflicting kinds of things. Everything in life that has any significance comes in paradox.

How can one thing be two opposites and still be one thing? How can a human being be someone who wants love and wants to get it, *chases* love, and never gets it? The person who doesn't obsess about getting love but just *is* love has love come into their life.

MARCH I

Surrender to a new consciousness, a thought that whispers, *I can do this thing in this moment. I will receive all the help I need as long as I stay with this intention and go within for assistance.*

MARCH 2

It is my contention that the bigger the purpose we signed up for in life, the bigger and harder the falls we encounter will be. I came here to accomplish big things, you see; therefore, I am not at all surprised when the challenges and the falls come in big doses. In fact, I now feel that any big challenge is an opportunity to grow to a higher spiritual level, where gratitude gradually replaces remorse.

MARCH 3

Your vast intelligence isn't measurable by an IQ test, nor is it susceptible to the analysis of school transcripts. Your ideas or beliefs about what you'd like to be, accomplish, or attract are evidence of your genius. If you're capable of conceiving it, then that act of visual conception, combined with your passion for manifesting your idea into reality, is all you need to activate your genius.

MARCH 4

To be attached to your physical appearance is to ensure a lifetime of suffering as you watch your form go through the natural motions that began the moment of your conception.

MARCH 5

Practice being a living, breathing paradox every moment of your life. The body has physical boundaries—it begins and ends and has material substance. Yet it also contains something that defies boundaries, has no substance, and is infinite and formless. Let the contrasting and opposite ideas be within you at the same time. Allow yourself to hold those opposite thoughts without them canceling each other out. Believe strongly in your free will and ability to influence your surroundings, and simultaneously surrender to the energy within you. Know that good and evil are two aspects of a union. In other words, accept the duality of the material world while still remaining in constant contact with the oneness of the eternal Tao.

MARCH 6

The choice is up to you: It can either be "Good morning, God!" or "Good God, morning."

MARCH 7

The more you attach your value and humanity to those things outside yourself, the more you give those things the power to control you.

MARCH 8

Each of the components of ego make entirely different demands than our Source of being does. Spirit calls us home to a perfect alignment with our Creator; ego is moving at high speed in the opposite direction. We must get better acquainted with Spirit if we wish to make a U-turn while we're still alive . . . and fully experience the afternoon of life.

❖

MARCH 9

The labeling process is what most of us were taught in school. We studied hard to be able to define things correctly in order to get what we called "high grades." Most educational institutions insisted on identifying everything, leading to a tag that distinguished us as graduates with knowledge of specific categories. Yet we know, without anyone telling us, that there is no title, degree, or distinguishing label that truly defines us. In the same way that water is not the word *water*—any more than it is *agua, Wasser,* or H_2O—nothing in this universe is what it's named. In spite of our endless categorizations, each animal, flower, mineral, and human can never truly be described. In the same way, the Tao tells us that "the name that can be named is not the eternal name." We must bask in the magnificence of what is seen and sensed, instead of always memorizing and categorizing.

MARCH 10

Death is a concept that refers to endings. Endings need boundaries, and your dimensionless self has no boundaries.

MARCH 11

Ego-fixated wants can get in the way of Divine essence, so practice getting ego out of the way and be guided by the Tao in all that you do. In a state of frenzy? Trust in the Tao. Listen for what urges you onward, free from ego domination, and you'll paradoxically be more productive. Allow what's within to come forward by suspending worldly determination. In this way, it will no longer be just you who is conducting this orchestration that you call your life.

❖

MARCH 12

Those who injured us only did what they knew how to do, given the conditions of their lives. If you won't forgive, then you allow those ancient injuries to continue their hold on you.

❖

MARCH 13

If you're still following a career path that you decided upon as a young person, ask yourself this question today: *Would I seek out the advice of a teenager for vocational guidance?*

MARCH 14

Be a good animal and move freely, unencumbered with thoughts about where you *should* be and how you *should* be acting. For instance, imagine yourself as an otter just living your "otterness." You're not good or bad, beautiful or ugly, a hard worker or a slacker . . . you're simply an otter, moving through the water or on the land freely, peacefully, playfully, and without judgments. When it's time to leave your body, you do so, reclaiming your place in the pure mystery of oneness.

MARCH 15

Have in your mind that which would constitute a miracle for you. Get the vision. Suspend disbelief and skepticism.

MARCH 16

Awareness takes you out of your customary thinking. Since rewiring my thoughts to influence my body and even my DNA, my reality has changed significantly. Today when I feel a heaviness in my chest or get a sore throat, a pain in my joints, or even a headache, I first begin noticing without judgment. I simply pay attention by observing uncritically and allowing myself to focus in a curious, gentle manner. When I turn toward my higher self, all of ego's fear begins fading in its light. When I become aware— without falling into ego thoughts of pain, disruption, and annoyance, or creating other mental barriers— the symptoms move on through my system, which is in a state of higher consciousness.

MARCH 17

Just as each flower has its own unique color—
even though it originates from only one light—each
individual, although unique in appearance, comes
from one essence as well.

MARCH 18

If you find your worldly ego interpreting or judging, then just observe that without criticizing or changing it. You'll begin to find more and more situations where it feels peaceful and joyful to *be* without response . . . just to be in the infinity that's hidden but always present.

You might want to duplicate this advice of my teacher Nisargadatta Maharaj and post it conspicuously so that you can read it daily: *Wisdom is knowing I am nothing, love is knowing I am everything, and between the two my life moves.*

And while you're living, stay as close to love as you can.

MARCH 19

We talk privately to God and call it prayer. So, then, why does a return call seem so far-fetched, particularly if we believe that there's some universal intelligence out there that we're addressing?

MARCH 20

Purpose is about giving yourself unconditionally and accepting what comes back with love, even if what comes back isn't what you'd anticipated.

MARCH 21

No one can depress you. No one can make you anxious. No one can hurt your feelings. No one can make you anything other than what you allow inside.

MARCH 22

Nothingness is equivalent to the expression of zero, mathematically: It can't be divided; it has no empirical value; and if we multiply anything by it, we get a sum of nothing. Yet without the indivisible zero, mathematics itself would be impossible. Before we came into this material world, our essence was nothing. We had no things encumbering us—no rules, no duties, no money, no parents, no hunger, no fear . . . nothing at all.

MARCH 23

A few minutes spent in total awe will contribute to your spiritual awakening faster than any metaphysics course.

MARCH 24

Throughout life, the two most futile emotions are guilt for what *has* been done, and worry about what *might* be done.

MARCH 25

In one magically mysterious nanosecond, we made the transition from nonbeing to being. A subatomic particle of human protoplasm emerged from Spirit, and everything that was needed for the journey we call life was taken care of. An invisible force that I call a future-pull was set in motion, filling in our physical characteristics. Our ultimate height; body shape; eye, skin, and hair color; wrinkles that would someday appear; and, of course, the business of our body ceasing to be alive, were all arranged, without our having to do a thing about it.

MARCH 26

Chasing success is like trying to squeeze a handful of water. The tighter you squeeze, the less water you get. When you chase it, your life becomes the chase, and you become a victim of always wanting more.

MARCH 27

You can sit there forever, lamenting about how bad you've been, feeling guilty until you die, and not one tiny slice of that guilt will do anything to change anything in the past.

MARCH 28

If you're committed to seeing your physical self with wonder and awe, and if you can know deep within that your invisible self wants the body it inhabits to be as healthy as possible, then you're a student who is ready.

MARCH 29

That which offends you only weakens you. Being offended creates the same destructive energy that offended you in the first place—so transcend your ego and stay in peace.

MARCH 30

Allow yourself to enjoy silence and meditation. Even if you don't have a structured meditation practice, give yourself time to simply savor the silence. Turn off the noisemakers at home and in your auto. Create time to be in nature away from human-made sounds. Learn to treat your voyages inward as sacred space, spending moments repeatedly letting go by physically and mentally relaxing. Let go of worrying, planning, thinking, recalling, wondering, hoping, desiring, or remembering. Consciously let go of each physical sensation you notice. Do this one moment at a time. Enter a state where you can let your possessions, your family, your home, your work, and your body cease to exist. Experience the inner bliss of nothingness.

When you emerge from your silence, begin the process of detachment by literally giving away something that you don't use at least once every day. In nothingness, you will find greater intimacy with your Source of being.

MARCH 31

Believing that there's a shortage of prosperity is a signal to think in terms of the inexhaustible Source: the Tao. Just like everything else on our planet, money is available in limitless quantities. Know this and connect to the bottomless supply. Do it first in your thoughts by affirming: *Everything I need now is here.* Prosperity thoughts are energetic instructions to access your infinite self, so actions will follow them.

APRIL 1

I once got two letters about the same book: One said that it was the greatest book that he had ever read—it had changed his life completely—and gave me all of the credit for his transformation. The other one said, "The book is so bad that I insist you send me a refund."

Here's what I did with the letters: I sent the nice one to the guy who wrote me the bad letter, and I sent the bad one to the guy who had written the good letter. And I wrote to each the great line that H. L. Mencken always used to send to opinionated letter writers: "You may be right."

Not "I'm right, and you're wrong." Just "You may be right." These two contrasting letters show how wasteful it is to be consumed by what other people think. What other people think is just that: they "may be right."

APRIL 2

If you would like to become a person who has the capacity to have all of your wishes fulfilled, it will be necessary for you to move to that higher plane of existence where you are a co-creator of your life. This means that you'll need to undertake what is often presumed to be the difficult task of changing your concept of yourself. Your concept of yourself is everything you believe to be true about your inner and outer self. Those beliefs have created the life you're now living—at what I call an ordinary level of awareness. To move into "extraordinary space" requires you to change what you believe is true.

APRIL 3

I recommend being gentle with yourself and loving yourself unconditionally, regardless of what comes your way.

APRIL 4

Every self-limiting thought that you employ to explain why you're not living life to the absolute fullest—so you're feeling purposeful, content, and fully alive—is something you can challenge and reverse, regardless of how long you've held that belief and no matter how rooted in tradition, science, or life experience it may be. Even if it seems like an insurmountable obstacle, you can overcome these thoughts, and you can begin by noticing how they've been working to hold you back. Then you can embark on a deprogramming effort that allows you to live an excuse-free life, one day at a time, one miracle at a time, one new belief at a time!

APRIL 5

By letting go, you let God; and even more significantly, you become more like God and less like the ego,
with its lifetime practice of **e**dging **G**od **o**ut.

APRIL 6

It might sound contradictory to plan on being surprised, but everyone reports that quantum moments are unexpected, uninvited, and unforeseen. This is when synchronicity and serendipity collaborate to astound us. It's as if we surrender and let ourselves be *lived* by life. We become the student who is ready, and the teacher does in fact appear. However, this is generally preceded by a fall.

APRIL 7

Overvaluing possessions and accomplishments stems from our ego's fixation on getting *more*—wealth, belongings, status, power, or the like. The Tao recommends refraining from this kind of discontented way of life, which leads to thievery, contentiousness, and confusion. Rather than seeking more, the Tao practice of gratitude is what leads us to the contented life. We must replace personal desires with the Tao-centered question: *How may I serve?* By simply changing these kinds of thoughts, we will begin to see major changes taking place in our lives.

APRIL 8

Meditation gives you an opportunity to come to know your invisible self.

APRIL 9

Rather than put a label on yourself as Christian, Jew, Muslim, Buddhist, or whatever, instead make a commitment to be Christlike, Godlike, Mohammed-like, and Buddha-like.

❖

APRIL 10

    Inventory your desires and then turn them over to the unnameable. Yes, turn them over and do nothing but trust. At the same time, listen and watch for guidance, and then connect yourself to the perfect energy that sends whatever is necessary into your life. You (meaning your ego) don't need to do anything. Instead, allow the eternal perfection of the Tao to work through you.

❖

APRIL 11

We become what we think about all day long—this is one of the greatest secrets that so many people are unaware of as they live out their life mission. What we think about is the business of our minds. If that inner invisibleness called our mind is closed to new ideas and infinite possibilities, it is equivalent to killing off the most important aspect of our very humanity. A mind that is open and unattached to any one particular way of being or living is like having an empty container that can allow new and endless possibilities to enter and be explored.

APRIL 12

The power of your beliefs to keep you stuck is enormous. Those deeply ingrained notions act as chains restricting you from experiencing your unique destiny. You have the capacity to loosen these chains and make them work for, rather than against, you, to the point that you can alter what you thought were scientific explanations for your human limitations and characteristics. I'm referring to things such as your genetic makeup; your DNA; or the early conditioning imposed upon you when you were an embryo, infant, and young child. Yes, you read that correctly. *Your beliefs, all of those formless energy patterns that you've adopted as your self-image, have the ability to change dramatically and give you the power to conquer unwanted traits, or what you unhappily presume to be your fate.*

APRIL 13

Buckminster Fuller said that 99 percent of who we are as human beings you can't touch, and you can't see, and you can't feel, and you can't smell. You can't get hold of it. It's the part of us that is in "nonform" that we can only define as thought, or mental imagery, or visualization, or feelings, or words that defy a formula, because there's no form to them.

The rules are different in this part of our consciousness, this 99 percent. But we are obsessed with the one percent. The one percent that is in form. We spend most of our energy in the one percent, looking at each other's packages.

APRIL 14

Conflict cannot survive without your participation.

APRIL 15

When acknowledged as a sign of change, worry is transitory—it's simply part of the world of the changing. If you view your life from the vantage point of an infinite observer, concerns, anxieties, and struggles blend into the eternal mix. From this ageless perspective, picture how important the things you feel depressed about now will be in a hundred, a thousand, a million, or an uncountable number of years. Remember that you, like the infinite Tao from which you originated, are part of an eternal reality.

APRIL 16

One song! That is our *uni* (one) *verse* (song). No matter how we separate into individual notes, we're all still involved in the one song.

APRIL 17

When you call yourself a jerk, that's your invisible critic judging your outer self. Remember, what you think about expands.

APRIL 18

Live in-Spirit. You came from Spirit, and to be inspired you must become more like where you came from. You must live so as to become more like God.

APRIL 19

God will work *with* you, not *for* you.

APRIL 20

The belief that we cannot change our biology is beginning to be challenged by scientific scholars engaged in cell-biology research. It seems that humans *do* have the ability to change and even reverse some of their genetic blueprints. Openness and curiosity, along with a desire to be free from excuses, are the basic prerequisites for learning about the exciting evidence concerning genetic predisposition.

APRIL 21

Forgiveness is the ability to give love away in the most difficult of circumstances.

APRIL 22

The more you try to force something for your own benefit, the less you'll enjoy what you're seeking so desperately.

APRIL 23

I've been looking at my hand lately. Take a look at your hand. Now, if I thought *that* was me, I'd freak out. You've got all these veins and all these nails, and you lay it all out. Everything that constitutes form. And you get it all there, and you say, "*That* is a human being."

That's not a human being! How *can* that be? Is that all you are, just gristle and bone? All that stuff, all that form? Where's your mind? That isn't in there. How do you account for that?

What is that thing that constitutes you being a human? Because you could find all of this in a pig or a horse. All of that—every bit of it—you'll find in a horse. There's something else that constitutes your humanity. That something else is *all that you are.*

APRIL 24

Why not think about some things you've never done before and do them simply because you've never done them and for no other reason?

APRIL 25

There exists within all of us a Divine spark, called
the *I am that I am*, and when it is kindled and nourished,
it is capable of miracle-making at an astonishing level.

APRIL 26

I believe in miracles, and I also know that I am not
this outer body. I have no fear of death because I am
birthless, deathless, and changeless. This is my *I am*
presence of being one with God.

APRIL 27

Human beings are multidimensional. We don't get that. We think we're just one-dimensional, maybe two-. We don't see that there are eighteen, twenty, fifty, *hundreds* of dimensions that are all part of this transitional process called humanity.

And when you get that, death is no longer anything to be terrified of. It's not about belief or faith; it isn't a religious thing. It's just an understanding that you can't kill thought.

APRIL 28

Being a spiritual being involves being able to touch your invisible self.

APRIL 29

Failure is a judgment, an opinion. It stems from your fears, which can be eliminated by love—love for yourself, love for what you do, love for others, and love for your planet.

APRIL 30

There's a level of awareness available to you that you are probably unfamiliar with. It extends upward and transcends the ordinary level of consciousness that you're most accustomed to. At this higher plane of existence, which you and every human being who has ever lived can access at will, the fulfillment of wishes is not only probable—it is guaranteed.

MAY 1

The ideal of your soul, the thing that it yearns for, is not more knowledge. It is not interested in comparison, nor winning, nor light, nor ownership, nor even happiness. The ideal of your soul is space, expansion, and immensity, and the one thing it needs more than anything else is to be free to expand, to reach out and to embrace the infinite. Why? Because your soul is infinity itself. It has no restrictions or limitations—it resists being fenced in—and when you attempt to contain it with rules and obligations, it is miserable.

MAY 2

Each place along the way is somewhere you had to be in order to be here.

❖

MAY 3

You have to take responsibility for everything that you are in your life and everything that you live internally. Now the word *responsibility*, to me, means "responding with ability." It doesn't mean "responding with disability"; otherwise, the word would be *respon-disability*. It is *responsibility*. I have the ability to respond. I can respond with ability.

❖

❖

MAY 4

Your self-concept is a blend of your beliefs regarding your connection to a higher power. You believe something about the existence or nonexistence of God. You have various points of view about how far faith can carry you. Whether or not there is anything within you that you can or cannot rely on to perform mystical or miraculous things is seasoned by your beliefs. You have acquired specific beliefs concerning the power of your mind. You're generally confident that you can rely on your invisibleness to do the ordinary things in life, such as remember an unseen list of items stored somewhere in your memory, and run errands on your way home from work. But what do your beliefs cook up about your ability to create *miracles*? Is healing your body, or manifesting a long-desired soul mate, an ingredient in your self-concept?

❖

❖

MAY 5

In childhood, repetition was something you most likely used to reinforce things you were mastering. (You can probably recall insisting on someone reading and rereading a book or story until you knew it by heart.) In that spirit, repeat this affirmation over and over to have it solidify, and move from your subconscious, habitual mind to the forefront of your conscious mind: *I let go of old ways of thinking, and I access awareness.*

❖

❖

MAY 6

When you judge others, you don't define them—
you define *yourself*.

❖

MAY 7

There seem to be unseen forces that direct me as I move forward on my spiritual path, fulfilling a dharma that Carl Jung also expressed about his life's work. Like him, I've often felt that "sense of destiny, as though my life was assigned to me by fate and had to be fulfilled." Throughout my entire professional career, when I've felt tugged toward a newer and a higher spiritual place, I too have felt guided. It's as if angels send me information related to what I will be writing and experiencing—long before the actual writing/speaking.

MAY 8

Learn to find the blessing in pain. Practice *observing* the pain, rather than owning it.

◆

MAY 9

Once you've learned how to enter your inner kingdom, you have a special retreat within that's always available to you.

◆

❖

MAY 10

As I began my eighth decade here on planet Earth, I found myself looking back at the more notable influences in my life that seemed to just *show up*. From this distance, I could see the impact they had in reversing the ego-dominated direction my life was taking at those earlier times. When these exceptional signal events or people materialized in my past, I was unable, as most of us are unable at the time, to access the larger perspective of what was happening. Now, from this perspective of looking back and writing about how to live a wishes-fulfilled life from a spiritual vantage point, I see those events as the pieces of a puzzle in a grand tapestry that is awe-inspiring and very meaningful to me today.

❖

MAY 11

You can't get hold of the wind. It's the same with thought.

MAY 12

Allow yourself to become aware of the nonphysical reality that you are a part of. Reach out to the angels or occupants of this higher invisible plane. Know that you can access guidance from those who've lived here before. Spend time in meditation accessing the feelings of a plane of higher consciousness.

MAY 13

Yesterday is just as over as the Peloponnesian War.

MAY 14

In the world of form, blame is a convenient excuse for why our world is not exactly what we'd like it to be. The state of the world is a reflection of our state of mind.

MAY 15

You'll come to find that anything you *must* have comes to own you. The funny thing is, when you release it, you start getting more of it.

MAY 16

Are you part of the problem or part of the solution?

MAY 17

I'm reminded of Henry David Thoreau's observation that "our truest life is when we are in dreams awake." It seems only logical to me that if during one-third of our life on planet Earth, we are capable of manifesting anything that we place our attention on—without having to expend any physical effort, only by allowing ourselves to transcend time and space—then why not in the other two-thirds of our life? This is what I believe Thoreau is suggesting when he urges us to be true to our authentic self by being a waking dreamer.

MAY 18

A higher concept of yourself involves taking on new truths and shedding your old views of what you can achieve. This is the only way you can achieve your desires.

MAY 19

Always remember that each day as you look at your world and see millions upon millions of flowers opening up, God does it all without using any force.

MAY 20

You begin this exciting adventure of changing your concept of yourself by being willing to die to your present self. That's right, by relinquishing your personal history as the arbiter of your life, you cease to resist your fuller potential. You simply no longer choose to form your identity on the basis of what you've been taught. Remind yourself that everything you've believed to be true has brought you to this point where you want to *explore* rather than *resist* your higher powers.

MAY 21

In order to forgive, you must have blamed. Ultimately, there's nothing to forgive, because there's nothing to judge and no one to blame.

MAY 22

Be patient and loving with every fearful thought. Practice observing your fears as a witness and you'll see them dissolve.

MAY 23

Remind yourself often that you have to send the old unworkable fabrications about your highest self out of your life forever. Be able to say, "I am God," with pride and assurance that you are not being blasphemous or inappropriate. Believing in that ego-driven idea of God as a malevolent superbeing who plays favorites and is filled with rage if you displease Him is akin to believing in the Easter bunny and praying to that rabbit to solve your problems. Keep uppermost in your thoughts the words of Jesus—"God is love"—and that you are proud to be that all-powerful God yourself.

All your doubts are obstacles inhibiting your entry into the kingdom of real magic.

MAY 25

The most important thing we can do to defuse the influence of ego is to proclaim ourselves *ready*! Remember the ancient saying that instructs: "When the student is ready, the teacher will appear." The teachers and teachings are always there, throughout the entire span of our life. But when ego is running things, those teachers go unnoticed. Once we truly acknowledge our readiness to live a life on purpose and filled with meaning, there's very little to do. We begin living in a different world than we experience in our ego-directed persona. As I've written and said many times: *When we change the way we look at things, the things we look at change.*

MAY 26

You see what you believe, rather than believe what you see.

MAY 27

Your imagination can undergo a complete overhaul. Replace the old ideas of *I've always been this way, It's my nature, It's the only thing I've ever known,* with *I am God, I am capable, I am strong, I am wealthy, I am healthy, I am happy.* Use your imagination for the fulfillment of all your God-realized and God-aligned wishes. Expand your imagination beyond the concept of yourself that limits you to ordinary consciousness.

MAY 28

You are at once a beating heart and a single heart-beat in this body called humanity.

MAY 29

It's impossible to pick up on what universal Source energy is transmitting if you stay misaligned and don't change frequencies to tune in to it. Just sit for a moment and let these thoughts be received right now: *You came from a Source that has unlimited abundance. It is still generating that same idea today—you merely left it behind. But when you return to those frequencies of your Source, you'll start to recognize them again. They'll begin to sound familiar to you. And ultimately you'll be back in harmony, singing the music that you sang long before you acquired an ego and began your journey of misalignment.*

MAY 30

An inner knowing, along with a burning desire, is the prerequisite for becoming a person capable of manifesting his or her heart's desires.

MAY 31

Quantum moments that turn life upside down are extremely intense. Even to this day, I can recall every detail of that spectacular quantum moment that occurred when I gave up alcohol. The sheets on the bed, the clothes hanging over the top of my closet door, a little cartoon taped to a mirror above my dresser, the container of coins on the floor, the color of the walls, a scratch mark on my headboard . . . everything is as vivid to me today as it was more than 20 years ago. It seems to me that when Spirit calls, it creates an exclamation point to emphasize the entire episode. There's a vividness that stays with us forever.

JUNE 1

You must first love yourself and be filled with love in order to be able to give it away. Once you are filled with that love and it is all that you have inside of you, then that is all that you will have to give away.

JUNE 2

A tree allows the life force to work naturally through it. You have the power within your thoughts to be as natural as the tree.

JUNE 3

You can quite readily break the habit of using your resting time before sleep reviewing things that are frustrating and upsetting. Make this a sacred, satisfying time to nurture thoughts that align with the *I am* thoughts that you have placed into your imagination. When you see a tendency toward negativity, simply pause and gently remind yourself in your sleepy state that you do not wish to enter your unconscious world with these feelings. Then assume that feeling in your body of your wish fulfilled. You want to enter your sleep with reminders to your subconscious to automatically fulfill your life-enhancing wishes.

JUNE 4

When you're told that you have some kind of physical affliction, you can either prepare to suffer or prepare to heal.

JUNE 5

If you want to find your true purpose in life, know this for certain: Your purpose will only be found in service to others, and in being connected to something far greater than your body/mind/ego.

JUNE 6

Keep in mind Saint Paul's words. There is a power in the universe that is able to go way beyond all that you could ever ask or even think, and it *works in you*. What else could this be other than your own imagination? Stay in a state of grace and gratitude for this resplendent gift that is always yours to do with as you choose.

JUNE 7

Don't equate your self-worth with how well you do things in life. You aren't what you do. If you are what you do, then when you *don't* . . . you *aren't*.

JUNE 8

Look at what you desire to bring into your life; then, feel grateful for everything you encounter. Express gratitude by riding the flow of your existence and allowing it to be your ally. You can steer while still enjoying this glorious ride, but if you elect to fight it, you'll ultimately get pulled under by its current. This is true for every aspect of your life: The more you push against it, the more resistance you create.

JUNE 9

Stop judging and get out of your own way. I always tell audiences when I talk about writing: Writing isn't something I do; writing is something that I am. I am writing—it's just an expression of me.

JUNE 10

The qualities of creativity and genius are within you, awaiting your decision to match up with the power of intention. Genius is a characteristic of the creative force that allows all of material creation to come into form. It is an expression of the Divine.

JUNE 11

Let go of your ego's need to be right. When you're in the middle of an argument, ask yourself: *Do I want to be right or be happy?* When you choose the joyous, loving, spiritual mode, your connection to intention is strengthened.

JUNE 12

The word *transformation* has the word *form* right smack in the middle, preceded by *trans*—meaning going beyond form. Live from the place that will indeed take you way beyond the limits of your seemingly limited life. Explore imagination, which is the Source of all being or physical reality.

JUNE 13

Alcohol, as well as all drugs (legal and otherwise),
lowers your body's energy level and weakens you.
In addition, you'll find that people with similar low
energy show up in your life. By retreating from these
substances, you can achieve the level of consciousness
you crave.

JUNE 14

I'm grateful to all those people who said no. It's because of them that I did it all myself.

JUNE 15

Invite the mysterious unseen world of Spirit to guide you. Create an atmosphere of allowing it in without pushing it. It all comes from Spirit, and your own imagination is Spirit itself if you stay aligned with the unseen.

JUNE 16

Look upon every experience you've ever had, and everyone who's ever played any role in your life, as having been sent to you for your benefit. In this universe, which was created by a Divine, organizing intelligence, there are simply no accidents.

JUNE 17

I spent years studying the teachings of Patanjali, and he reminded us several thousand years ago that when we are steadfast—which means that we never slip in our abstention of thoughts of harm directed toward others—then all living creatures cease to feel enmity in our presence. Now I know that we are all human: you, me, all of us. We do occasionally slip and retreat from our highest self into judgment, criticism, and condemnation, but this is not a rationale for choosing to practice that kind of interaction. I can only tell you that when I finally got it, and I sent only love to another of God's children whom I had been judging and criticizing, I got the immediate result of inner contentment.

JUNE 18

The concept of your *higher self* will gradually evolve into your *highest self*, which is truly omniscient, almighty, and capable of producing miracles. Here you will see a new reality—a majestic idea of yourself that previously seemed inconceivable.

JUNE 19

I write without doing. I simply allow ideas to come through me and onto the page. I'm not busy writing, trying, struggling, working, or any other *doing*—I'm simply letting go and letting God, just as I do with my heart, my lungs, my circulatory system, and everything else that the physical me comprises. I let myself be.

JUNE 20

The more you stop to observe animals and learn from them, the healthier and more peaceful your life will be.

JUNE 21

Choose to be in close proximity to people who are empowering, who appeal to your sense of connection to intention, who see the greatness in you, who feel connected to God, and who live a life that gives evidence that Spirit has found celebration through them.

◆

JUNE 22

Your higher self is a piece of an all-loving, all-embracing creative Source. All you need do is accept that this is not something external to yourself. It resides within you (the kingdom of Heaven is within)—in fact, it *is* you—and all you need do is begin to align with this Divine essence, begin to act like it acts and think like it thinks, and you will begin the process of manifesting just as it does.

◆

JUNE 23

Quality rather than appearance . . . ethics rather than rules . . . integrity rather than domination . . . knowledge rather than achievement . . . serenity rather than acquisitions.

JUNE 24

When you place an intention in your imagination, do not allow a question mark at the end of your pronouncement. See your statement ending in a grammatical exclamation point. "I bring this into my reality!" is easy to say if you're already living from that declaration in your imagination and have assumed the feeling in your body of that wish being fulfilled.

JUNE 25

If you don't love yourself, nobody else will. Not only that—you won't be good at loving anyone else. Loving starts with the self.

JUNE 26

The subconscious mind accepts as true what you feel is true. Your feelings determine your reality because they're impressed on the subconscious. Consciously feeling hopeless, and entertaining this idea in your imagination with even more imaginative feelings of hopelessness, will impress on the subconscious mind the idea of failure. Consequently, you will be offered experiences by the one universal subconscious mind that will match what you've felt is true. Remember, the subconscious mind is impersonal and nonselective. It cannot make a distinction between what you feel as a result of your daily life experiences and what you feel as a result of what you have placed into your imagination as a future desire.

JUNE 27

The first step toward discarding a scarcity mentality involves giving thanks for everything that you are and everything that you have.

JUNE 28

I can come up with a long list of reasons why I should be judgmental and condemnatory toward another of God's children and why, damn it, I am right. Yet if I want to perfect my own world—and I so want to do so—then I must substitute love for these judgments, or take the consequences of not having my wishes fulfilled.

JUNE 29

Highly realized people learn to think from the end—that is, they experience what they wish to intend before it shows up in material form. You can do the same by synchronizing with the power of intention.

JUNE 30

The subconscious mind possesses the power to manifest physical reality from thought. Every object and circumstance in this world is representative of a mental thought. *All that now exists was once imagined*—such is the power of the subconscious mind. But in order to partake of this incredible powerhouse of creation that you are, you must be able and willing to experience within yourself—in your mind—that which you wish to manifest. Thoughts become things when you *feel* them, and are able to impress them upon the subconscious mind, which will then take over.

JULY 1

Remember the truth I've written about many times:
You do not attract what you want; you attract what you are.

JULY 2

Are you willing to internalize radical new ideas that require a shift in your concept of yourself? Are you receptive to the idea of having a higher self that isn't defined by ego concerns? Are you able to entertain the idea of an unlimited higher self that is within you? Can you imagine that you can eschew ego's limiting demands that are keeping you stuck at an ordinary level of consciousness? In other words, can you approach the question of "Who am I?" with complete unknowing?

JULY 3

The more you see yourself as what you'd like to become, and act as if what you want is already there, the more you'll activate those dormant forces that will collaborate to transform your dream into your reality.

JULY 4

When you acquire enough inner peace and feel really positive about yourself, it's almost impossible for you to be controlled and manipulated by anybody else.

JULY 5

The pathway from nonbeing or Spirit to the world of an *Excuses Begone!* existence originates in your imagination. I love to remind myself of this mind-blowing idea: *An infinity of forests lies dormant within the dreams of one acorn.* Even a forest needs a vision, a dream, an idea; indeed, a fertile imagination.

JULY 6

You can't go around being what everyone expects
you to be, living your life through other people's rules,
and be happy and successful.

JULY 7

The more you extend kindness to yourself, the more it will become your automatic response to others.

JULY 8

You're someone who came here to fulfill a personal dharma, so let that genius gift from God finally be active in your life. Everything you need to fulfill your destiny was with you at the moment before, during, and after your conception—so retreat to that knowledge now.

JULY 9

You are in a partnership with all other human beings, not a contest to be judged better than some and worse than others.

JULY 10

If you want to be confident but don't normally act that way, then today, just this once, act in the physical world the way you believe a confident person would.

JULY 11

When you feel dejected or out of sorts, ask yourself: *Do I wish to use the present moment—the precious currency of my life—in this manner?* This will help you to become conscious of the importance of being here now—not just in your body, but in your thinking as well. I urge you to think of the present as just that: a wondrous present from your Source. Anytime you're filling the now with thoughts about how you used to be, concerns about what someone has done to harm you, or worries about the future, you're saying "No, thank you" to your Source for this precious gift.

JULY 12

Forgiveness is humanity's highest achievement because it shows true enlightenment in action. It shows that one is in touch with the energy of love.

JULY 13

Inspiration can be cultivated and be a driving enthusiasm *throughout* life, rather than showing up every now and then and just as mysteriously disappearing, seemingly independent of our desire. And it's *everyone's* Divine birthright—that is, it isn't reserved for high-profile creative geniuses in the arts and sciences. The problem is that from birth we're gradually taught to believe exclusively in the world ruled by Club Ego . . . and we put our full-time membership in Club Spirit on hold.

❖

JULY 14

Every thought that you have impacts you. By shifting in the middle of a weakening thought to one that strengthens, you raise your energy vibration and strengthen yourself and the immediate energy field.

❖

JULY 15

Judgment means that you view the world as *you* are, rather than as it is.

JULY 16

Rather than focusing on what you can't do because it's difficult and takes a long time, think like this: *This is definitely something that I can and will create for myself. I know I can do anything I put my mind to. I anticipate that this is within my ability to readily accomplish. I have no fear, because I recognize that whatever guidance and assistance I require is available. I'm excited, thrilled, and elated about fulfilling this dream. I realize that the thoughts I have are meshed with enthusiasm and passion, and that nothing can stop me. In fact, I'm certain that whatever I need to actualize my dreams is already on its way. I contentedly watch for what the universe sends me.*

JULY 17

The Law of Attraction proclaims that *like is attracted to like*. So when you think like the universal mind thinks, it will join you; when you think in ways that are antithetical to this Divine mind, you'll attract more of what you're thinking about. That means that if your thoughts are all focused on what's wrong, what's missing, what you can't do, or what you've never done before—that is, on *excuses*—you'll access more of what you're thinking about.

Use the Law of Attraction to say good-bye to excuses. When you do, the universe will recognize you, and help and guidance will show up in a synchronistic way. As you align with your authentic original self, rather than your ego, you'll start to feel as though you're collaborating with destiny.

◆

JULY 18

Your limits are defined by the agreement you've made about what's possible. Change that agreement and you can dissolve all limits.

◆

JULY 19

Whenever anyone has told me over the years that they just don't understand why I'm so "compulsive" about my health habits, I always think: *If I didn't have a healthy body, I wouldn't have anywhere to live.*

JULY 20

By referring to previous struggles and using them as reasons for not getting on with your life today, you're assigning responsibility to the past for why you can't be successful or happy in the present.

JULY 21

Remember to play with your imagination. Imagine that your brain is constructed in such a way that there's no excuse-making apparatus. So the moment you contemplate pursuing something you've always wanted to accomplish, your thoughts center around the idea that you possess boundless energy to do anything you put your mind to, and that you have plenty of time to pursue these activities.

JULY 22

You cannot always be number one, win a contest, get the merit badge, or make the honor roll, but you can always think of yourself as an important, worthwhile person.

JULY 23

We come from *no-where* to *now-here* with nothing.
We leave *now-here* for *no-where* with nothing. *No-where,*
now-here; it's all the same. It's just a question of spacing.

JULY 24

How do you determine that you're aligned with your soul's purpose? You know by the way the rational reason speaks directly to you in that personal place within. The thoughts and feelings that surface tend to go like this: *This is truly who I am. By making these changes and eradicating these excuses, I will be living my life on purpose, fulfilling a destiny I came here to accomplish.*

JULY 25

If you attempt to figure out how your Source of being thinks, the first thing you need to do is get rid of the ego. When you observe how creation takes place, you see that Source energy is all about *giving*, while your ego is all about *getting*. So aligning with Source energy means taking the focus off of *What's in it for me?* and shifting to *How may I serve?*

JULY 26

In order to get what you want, monitor your inner dialogue and match your thoughts to what you intend to create.

JULY 27

Some 2,500 years ago, Lao-tzu spoke of "the four cardinal virtues": *Reverence for All Life*, *Natural Sincerity*, *Gentleness*, and *Supportiveness*. He noted that when we practice them as a way of life, we come to know and access the truth of the universe. These four virtues don't represent external dogma, but a part of our original nature—by practicing them, we realign with Source and access the powers that Source energy has to offer. The more your life is harmonized with the four virtues, the less you're controlled by the uncompromising ego. And when your ego is tamed, you discover how easy it is to access Divine guidance—you and the Divine begin to operate on the same frequency.

❖

JULY 28

All of the "stuff" in your life has arrived to serve
you, rather than to make you a servant of the stuff.

❖

JULY 29

Eliminating lifelong thinking habits cannot and will not happen if it doesn't strike you as a sensible thing to do. It doesn't really matter that everyone you know tells you how important it is to change—if it doesn't make sense to you, then you'll retreat to your old ways and continue to explain them away with your convenient laundry list of excuses. If the answer to "Do I really want to bring about this change?" is yes, then that's all you need in order to proceed and succeed. But if you have any doubts whatsoever, your old excuse making will surface, and you'll revert back to your long-held habits.

JULY 30

Really examine your habits, along with all of the excuses you've adopted to explain yourself, and then ask yourself a simple question: *Do these make me feel good?* If the answer is no, then it's incumbent upon you to begin the process of making decisions that do in fact make you feel good. It's the same as aligning with the callings of your soul—because feeling good does indeed lift you into alignment with the callings of your soul.

JULY 31

Genuinely feeling abundant and successful is possible when you detach yourself from the things you desire and allow them to flow *to* you—and *through* you.

AUGUST 1

The reality is that beginnings are often disguised as painful endings. So when you know that there's a constant beyond the present moment's disappointment, you can sense that "this too shall pass"—it always has and always will.

AUGUST 2

Be aware of anything that's directing you toward activities that truly ignite your passion. If events seem to be taking you in a new direction in your work, for instance, or signs point to changing your job or location, pay attention! Don't get pulled under by refusing to budge and continuing a familiar frustrating routine, and then justifying your fear of change. Recognize the Tao energy coursing through your life and quit fighting your calling.

AUGUST 3

You can't get prune juice from an orange, no matter how hard you squeeze it. You can't give hate if you only have love inside.

AUGUST 4

The imbalance between your desire for a healthy body that feels great and persistently unhealthy habits is not remedied by simply changing those habits. You must have a firm determination to learn the art of passionately believing in something that doesn't yet exist, and refuse to allow that picture to be distorted by you or anyone else. Truly, you are not what you eat or how much you exercise, but rather what you believe about the you that you're presently birthing in your thoughts.

AUGUST 5

Co-creation is cooperatively using the energy from the invisible world of Spirit. It is perfectly balancing your in-the-world calling with the pure energy of creation.

AUGUST 6

One cannot choose sides on a round planet.

AUGUST 7

If you doubt the principles of the universe, they won't work for you.

AUGUST 8

By blaming God for not having what you need or desire, you justify a built-in excuse for accepting your lot in life. In reality, as Saint Paul reminds us, God is more than willing to provide you with the blessing of abundance. In fact, God *is* pure abundance, but *you* are the one out of balance on the prosperity scale. By putting the responsibility for your shortages on Divine will, you create enormous resistance energetically. You're asking the universe to send you more of what you believe in.

AUGUST 9

The concept of balance defines our universe. The cosmos, our planet, the seasons, water, wind, fire, and earth are all in perfect balance. We humans are the only exception. Getting in balance is not so much about adopting new strategies to change your behaviors as it is about realigning yourself in all of your thoughts so as to create a balance between what you desire and how you conduct your life on a daily basis.

AUGUST 10

You'll be happy to know that the universal law that created miracles hasn't been repealed.

AUGUST 11

What you think about expands. If your thoughts are centered on what's missing, then what's missing, by definition, will have to expand.

AUGUST 12

You come into this world in a wrinkled little body,
and you leave in a large wrinkled body . . . if you're lucky.

AUGUST 13

Since your mind is your own private territory, you can give any new idea a private audition for a few days before sharing it with others.

AUGUST 14

The whole universal system is held together through love, harmony, and cooperation. If you use your thoughts according to these principles, you can transcend anything that gets in your way.

❖

AUGUST 15

Begin to change your out-of-balance attitude by cultivating an inner affirmation until it becomes second nature. Silently repeat something similar to: *I am a piece of God, a Divine, individualized expression of God. I am worthy and deserving of all that God is and all that flows into my life. The abundance I desire is on its way, and I will do everything I can to avoid blocking and resisting this Divinely inspired flow.*

❖

AUGUST 16

Let go of the notion that things shouldn't be that way. They *are* that way!

AUGUST 17

You are water; water is you. Think about the mysterious magical nature of this liquid energy that we take for granted. If it stays stationary, it will become stagnant; if it is allowed to flow, it will stay pure. It does not seek the high spots to be above it all, but settles for the lowest places. It gathers into rivers, lakes, and streams; courses to the sea; and then evaporates to fall again as rain. It maps out nothing and it plays no favorites: It doesn't *intend* to provide sustenance to the animals and plants. It has no *plans* to irrigate the fields; to slake our thirst; or to provide the opportunity to swim, sail, ski, and scuba dive. These are some of the benefits that come naturally from water simply doing what it does and being what it is.

AUGUST 18

I can do virtually anything that I want to, because it isn't your form that counts. It isn't the age of your body that counts. It's whether you transcend your form. That's where *transformation* comes from.

Look at it this way: You've already occupied many different bodies on this planet. I mean, I was in an eight-pound body when I was born, and I was in a body that was only two and a half feet tall growing up. Nothing about me—not one physical cell—that was in my 10-year-old body is in the body that I carry now at 46. All has been changed, and yet I can remember everything about what I did when I was 10 years old, so I am not that body, which is now gone; I am the thoughts behind it. I am not a body with a soul; I'm a soul with a body.

AUGUST 19

Creating money is just like creating anything else
in your life: It involves not being attached to it, and not
giving it power over your life in any way.

AUGUST 20

If we are to have magical bodies, we must have magical minds.

AUGUST 21

Allow yourself to become aware of the nonphysical reality that you are a part of. Reach out to the angels or occupants of this higher invisible plane. Know that you can access guidance from those who've lived here before. Spend time in meditation accessing the feelings of a plane of higher consciousness.

AUGUST 22

Suffering is always played out in form. It is not you
who suffers, only the person you imagine yourself to be.

AUGUST 23

Why meditate? Anyone has at one time or another considered this question and come up with all sorts of answers. Some of the many reasons for meditating include reducing stress, cultivating a sense of peace, eliminating fatigue, slowing the aging process, improving memory, finding clarity of purpose, and even healing. All these are powerful motivators for beginning a meditation practice. Who *wouldn't* want the healthy, happy, and purposeful life that is the result of these benefits? However, all these reasons pale in significance compared to the realization that meditation is our way of making conscious contact with God.

AUGUST 24

If you're truly nonjudgmental, then it will be impossible for you to categorize or generalize individuals into groups such as: old, Southern, uneducated, teenyboppers, belonging to red or blue states, conservatives, liberals, and so on. A stereotype is a judgment—you cannot be nonjudgmental and be critical of the different ways people talk, eat, dress, socialize, dance, or anything else. If you believe that you're nonjudgmental but admit that you have a tendency to generalize and criticize, then you're out of balance! You're due for a realignment so that your current thoughts, and ultimately your behaviors, will become a vibrational match to your inner self-portrait.

AUGUST 25

You would never abuse something that you thought was very valuable. Suppose you had a beautiful vase that was worth $50,000—you would never abuse that. You wouldn't play catch with it, and you wouldn't throw it on the floor, would you? You would probably put it into some kind of safekeeping place where it couldn't be damaged.

Well, the same thing is true of yourself. If you think of yourself as very valuable, very important, very significant as a human being, then you would never, ever abuse yourself, and you wouldn't allow someone else to abuse you. Most abuse that people endure, whether it's their own smoking or overeating or alcoholism or whatever, comes from a belief, a fundamental belief, that *what I'm abusing isn't worth anything.*

❖

AUGUST 26

One of the huge imbalances in life is the disparity between your daily existence, with its routines and habits, and the dream you have deep within yourself of some extraordinarily satisfying way of living.

AUGUST 27

Overcoming the imbalance of addictive thinking begins and ends with your awareness that you, with the help of your Source, have everything you need right now to end your imbalance. As an ancient Hindu saying reminds us: "God gives food to every bird, but he doesn't throw it into the nest." Realign with God, and fly without the weight of addiction. I promise you that being in balance and free of addiction is much more exhilarating!

AUGUST 28

Love your addictions. If it's food, love it. If it's cig-arettes, love them. These are some of your greatest teachers. They've taught you through direct experi-ence what it is that you no longer wish to be. They've taken you to the depths for some reason. This is an intelligent system you're a part of. There are no acci-dents in a universe supported by omniscience and omnipotence. Be grateful for these teachers.

If you hate them, curse them, and attempt to fight these addictions, you tip the balance toward hatred and fighting. You then continue to chase after what you don't want because you're in a weakened state. Fighting weakens; love empowers.

So tip the scale toward love. Be grateful for the addictions that have taught you so much. Send them a silent blessing. By doing so, you shift toward the love that you are.

AUGUST 29

When we love ourselves, we refuse to allow others to manage our emotions from afar. Forgiveness is our means to that end.

AUGUST 30

The absence of balance between dreams and habits may be very subtle. It doesn't necessarily reveal itself in the obvious symptoms of heartburn, depression, illness, or anxiety—it's more often something that feels like an unwelcome companion by your side, which continually whispers to you that you're ignoring something. There's some often-unidentifiable task or experience that you sense is part of your beingness. It may seem intangible, but you can feel the longing to be what you're intended to be. You sense that there's a higher agenda; your *way of life* and your *reason for life* are out of balance. Until you pay attention, this subtle visitor will continue to prod you to regain your equilibrium.

AUGUST 31

I think you're better off tossing out your personal history of any deficiencies that have surfaced in your life. Refuse to think about what's failed to materialize unless you're hoping for more of the same. Avoid talking about your bleak past. Don't identify yourself as someone whose childhood or early adulthood was characterized by dearth and paucity. Instead, look upon your entire history as a series of steps you absolutely needed to take in order to bring you to the present realization of your endless potential for abundance.

SEPTEMBER 1

When you're overly involved with the physical, to the exclusion of the spiritual, you place a heavy emphasis on winning, becoming number one, and comparing yourself to others. A preoccupation with the material aspects of life leads to looking at life in a superficial way, where appearance is viewed as more important than substance. In fact, how it looks supersedes how it feels. What others think is the most important measuring device, and how you stack up to externally imposed standards becomes all-important.

SEPTEMBER 2

Giving is the key to forgiving.

SEPTEMBER 3

In any situation—whether it be under the heading of "family," "work," or "social," or even just seeing the atrocities reported on the evening news—you'll become aware that there's no "they" who have power over you. By refusing to turn the controls of your existence over to anyone or any set of circumstances, you're exercising personal strength instead of force. You are indeed experiencing self-mastery because you've elected to live in accordance with the Tao. You don't need the approval of others or another possession in order to be happy—you must merely understand yourself as a Divine piece of the eternal Tao, always connected to that infinite essence.

SEPTEMBER 4

Your inner candle flame, which symbolizes who you are as a human being, must never flicker. Your outer candle flame—representing all the things that can happen to you—you're not always in control of. Storms can happen, things can happen to your body, you can have accidents . . . any number of things. But your inner candle flame is yours. It's unique. You must get to the point where it doesn't flicker, regardless of what's going on out there.

SEPTEMBER 5

Everything is energy; it's all vibration at a variety of frequencies. The faster the vibration, the closer one is to Spirit. The pen I hold in my hand appears to be solid, yet it's actually a field of moving particles, with mostly empty space between those particles. The vibrational makeup of my pen is energy that is slow enough to appear solid to my eyes.

I hear the sounds of mynah birds as I write, and I know from the laws of physics that sounds are a faster energy than my solid pen. The light I see streaming in my window is an even faster energy, with tiny particles moving so fast as to appear to be green or blue or yellow, depending on how the rods and cones in my eyes are calibrated. Beyond the frequencies of light are the vibrational energies of thought.

SEPTEMBER 6

The dying process in the physical world allows you to live.

SEPTEMBER 7

Our individual thoughts create a prototype in the universal mind of intention. You and your power of intention are not separate. So, when you form a thought within you that's commensurate with Spirit, you form a spiritual prototype that connects you to intention and sets into motion the manifestation of your desires. Whatever you wish to accomplish is an existing fact, already present in Spirit. Eliminate from your mind thoughts of conditions, limitations, or the possibility of it not manifesting. If left undisturbed in your mind and in the mind of intention simultaneously, it will germinate into reality in the physical world.

SEPTEMBER 8

Your desire to be and live from greatness is an aspect of your spiritual energy. In order to create balance in this area of your life, you have to use the energy of your thoughts to harmonize with what you desire. Your mental energy attracts what you think about. Thoughts that pay homage to frustration will attract frustration. When you say or think anything resembling *There's nothing I can do; my life has spun out of control, and I'm trapped*, that's what you'll attract—that is, resistance to your highest desires! Every thought of frustration is like purchasing a ticket for more frustration. Every thought that agrees that you're stuck is asking the universe to send you even *more* of that glue to *keep* you stuck.

SEPTEMBER 9

Your miracles are an inside job. Go there to create the magic you seek in your life.

SEPTEMBER 10

You have a profound calling back to Spirit. It is working right now in your life. I urge you to heed that calling and come to know the pure bliss that awaits you as you make an inspired life your reality.

SEPTEMBER 11

Perhaps the most important question is: *How do you want to be perceived in this world?* Anyone who responds that they don't care at all is trying to live with blinders on—a rather unbalanced style, to be sure. Of course you care! In some cases, your very livelihood depends on your response to this question. You want to enjoy relating in a joyful, playful, intimate, loving, helpful, concerned, caring, and thoughtful manner with others. It's the nature of all of our human relationships to want to give and receive those emotions, and to feel connected to each other.

SEPTEMBER 12

Have a mind that is open to everything and attached to nothing.

SEPTEMBER 13

Find an opportunity to observe a tiny little green sprout emerging from a seed. When you do, allow yourself to feel the awe of what you're seeing. The scene of an emerging sprout represents the beginning of life. No one on this planet has even a tiny clue as to how all of this works. What is that creative spark that causes the life to sprout? What created the observer, the consciousness, the observation, and perception itself? The questions are endless.

SEPTEMBER 14

Positive thoughts keep you in harmony with the universe.

SEPTEMBER 15

That music that you hear inside of you urging you to take risks and follow your dreams is your intuitive connection to the purpose in your heart since birth. Be enthusiastic about all that you do. Have that passion with the awareness that the word *enthusiasm* literally means "the God (*entheos*) within (*iasm*)." The passion that you feel is God inside of you beckoning you to take the risk and be your own person.

SEPTEMBER 16

A mind at peace, a mind focused on not harming others, is stronger than any physical force in the universe.

SEPTEMBER 17

The willingness and ability to live fully in the now eludes many people. While eating your appetizer, don't be concerned with dessert. While reading a book, notice where your thoughts are. While on vacation, be there instead of thinking about what should have been done and what has to be done when returning home. Don't let the elusive present moment get used up by thoughts that aren't in the here and now.

SEPTEMBER 18

Pick a time today, perhaps between noon and 4 P.M., to consciously free your mind from attempting to control the events of your life. Go for a walk and simply let yourself be carried along: Let your feet go where they will. Observe everything in your line of vision. Notice your breath, the sounds you hear, the wind, the cloud formations, the humidity, the temperature—everything. Simply let yourself be immersed and transported, and notice how it feels to just go with the flow. Now decide to let freedom be your guide. Realize that traffic, the people in your life, the stock exchange, the weather, the tides . . . all of it is taking place at its own pace in its own way. You can move with the eternal, perfect Tao as well. *Be it* . . . now.

❖

SEPTEMBER 19

It is from out of the indivisible silence that creation flows, and this is where we can all make direct contact with our Source of being.

SEPTEMBER 20

Thoughts and emotions are pure energy; some higher and faster than others. When higher energies occupy the same field as lower energies, the lower energies convert to higher energies. A simple example of this is a darkened room that has lower energy than a room bathed in light. Since light moves faster than non-light, when a candle is brought into a dark room, the darkness not only dissolves and disappears, but it seems magically converted into light. The same is true of love, which is a higher/faster energy than the energy of hate.

SEPTEMBER 21

If you desire spiritual consciousness, then you need to be more in harmony with your spiritual Source. This is a Source of love, kindness, joy, beauty, nonjudgment, creativity, and endless abundance. If you think that you personify all of these qualities, yet everyone else perceives you in a totally different light, then it's likely that you're living an illusion and will continue to be in a state of imbalance.

SEPTEMBER 22

Make a deliberate decision to spend more time in the presence of those whom you're most closely aligned to in-Spirit. This means seeking out "higher-vibrational people" and avoiding those who reflect more ego-oriented behavior patterns. Keep in mind that higher spiritual energies nullify your lower tendencies, while also converting you to more in-Spirit frequencies. Use your own inner hunches to determine if you're in the right places with the right people: If you feel good in their presence, meaning that you feel inspired to be a better and more joyful person, then these are right for you. If, on the other hand, you feel more anxious, depressed, and uninspired, and you can't wait to get away because of conflict, then these are not going to be sources of inspiration for you.

SEPTEMBER 23

Having a plan isn't necessarily unhealthy, but falling in love with the plan is a real neurosis . . . don't let your plan become bigger than you are.

SEPTEMBER 24

As you integrate all of yourself, assembling the parts into the oneness that is you, you'll discover the impossibility of your being separate from anyone else on our planet. Simply recognizing the times of anger or annoyance as opportunities to know yourself better, and to forgive and love yourself, will extend your awareness of the oneness you are. Practice this kind of oneness, and love will flow outward naturally to include others whom you've previously judged.

SEPTEMBER 25

Every fall has within it the potential to move us to a higher place. It may be necessary to get down and dirty in the dark night of the soul in order to free ourselves from the grip of a well-established ego. "Hidden in all misfortune is good fortune" is a Tao concept that seems to support the value of those times in life when we've experienced a fall. Without that particular misfortune, good fortune is unavailable.

SEPTEMBER 26

In reality, it's much easier not to smoke or eat chocolate than to do so. It's your mind that convinces you otherwise.

SEPTEMBER 27

Begin looking at the world as a vast mirror reflecting back to you exactly what you are. If you truly are a loving human being, the world will look like a loving place to you, and this will be how you're perceived. You will have restored balance, and consequently, there will be no discrepancy between how you see yourself and what the world is reflecting back to you. If the world continues to look like an unloving and unlivable place, I urge you to keep examining the kind of energy that you're projecting outward.

SEPTEMBER 28

The Bhagavad Gita tells us: "We are born into the world of nature; our second birth is into the world of Spirit." Taming the influence of the ego is the beginning of that second birth. By taming the ego, we elicit the support and assistance of our originating Spirit, and we come to notice synchronicities happening in our life. The people we need appear, circumstances come together in a way that assists us on our dharma path, financing becomes available that was never there before, and so on.

SEPTEMBER 29

Awareness of the omnipresence of the Tao means that thoughts of shortages or lack aren't prevalent. Beliefs such as "There's no way this will happen," "It's not my destiny," or "With my luck, things could never work out," cease to be entertained. Instead, you begin to expect that what you imagine for yourself is not only on its way—it's already here! This new self-portrait based on the cooperative presence of the invisible Tao elevates you to living an inspired life—that is, one of being in-Spirit or in unending touch with the Tao. When you live infinitely, the rewards are a sense of peaceful joy because you know that all is in order.

SEPTEMBER 30

I abhor the concept of "failure." I never, ever wanted any of my children to think of themselves as having failed at anything. As they have heard me say on countless occasions, "There is no failure, only feedback—everything that you do produces a result. My only concern for you is what you do with the results you produce, rather than labeling yourself as a failure and then having to live with that label."

OCTOBER 1

How can anyone be a pessimist in a world where we know so little? A heart starts beating inside a mother's womb a few weeks after conception, and it's a total mystery to everyone on our planet. In comparison to what there is to know, we are only embryos. Keep this in mind whenever you encounter those who are absolutely certain that there's only one way to do something.

OCTOBER 2

Blaming others for one's misery means that you have to wait for the person you blamed to change before you can experience happiness. And that, of course, is a fool's errand. This is the opposite of self-reliance.

OCTOBER 3

Attachment to being right creates suffering. When you have a choice to be right or to be kind, choose kindness, and watch your suffering disappear.

OCTOBER 4

In the East, they contemplate the forest; in the West, they count the trees.

OCTOBER 5

In every single case of a person experiencing a spontaneous healing or overcoming something that was considered to be impossible, the individual went through a complete reversal of personality. They actually rewrote their own agreement with reality. To experience Godlike spontaneous miracles, you must have a sense of yourself as Godlike. The Scriptures say, "With God all things are possible." Now tell me, what does that leave out?

OCTOBER 6

Your inner and outer design is perfectly in balance with all things in the universe.

OCTOBER 7

To release attachments, you have to make a shift in how you view yourself. If your primary identification is with your body and your possessions, your ego is the dominant force in your life. If you can tame your ego sufficiently, you'll call upon your spirit to be the guiding force in your life. As a spiritual being, you can observe your body and be a compassionate witness to your existence. Your spiritual aspect sees the folly of attachments because your spiritual self is an infinite soul.

OCTOBER 8

An open mind allows you to explore and create and grow. A closed mind seals off any such creative explanation. Remember that progress would be impossible if we always did things the way we always have. The ability to participate in miracles—true miracles in your life—happens when you open your mind to your limitless potential. Refuse to allow yourself to have low expectations about what you're capable of creating. The greater danger is not that your hopes are too high and you fail to reach them; it's that they're too low and you *do*.

OCTOBER 9

Slow down . . . Take your time . . . Your work isn't terribly important. Your worldly duties aren't terribly important. Make your first and primary priority in your life *being in balance with the Source of Creation*. Become thoughtful in your slowed-down time, and invite the Divine to be known in your life. Being the peace you desire means becoming a relaxed person whose balance point doesn't attract anxiety and stress symptoms.

OCTOBER 10

You may indeed find yourself living a comfortable life when you don't follow your instincts. You pay your bills, fill out all of the right forms, and live a life of fitting in and doing it by the book. But it's a book that was written by somebody else. You're aware of that nagging companion saying to you, "This may look right, but does it *feel* right? Are you doing what you came here to do?"

OCTOBER 11

The difference between being unhappy and being a no-limit person is not in terms of whether or not you have problems. Every human being on this planet has problems that they have to face every day of their life. But the fully functioning person is someone who has a different attitude toward their problems. The no-limit person recognizes the potential for growth in every situation and doesn't approach the problem as if it should be something different. In other words, he doesn't go out into the rain and say, "It shouldn't be raining. How come it's raining? It's not supposed to be raining. It's March—they promised me that it wouldn't rain in March. It's not fair. It didn't rain last March."

OCTOBER 12

It's important that you live more spontaneously—you don't need to neatly wrap up each detail of your life. Understand this and you can travel without being attached to a plan that covers every possible scenario. Your inner light is more trustworthy than any guidebook, and it will point you in the direction that's most beneficial to you and everyone you encounter.

OCTOBER 13

Catch yourself in the midst of any utterance that reflects your belief that you're average. Silently speak warmly to that belief and ask it what it wants. It may think it has to protect you from disappointment or pain, as it probably did earlier in your existence. But with continued accepting attention, the feeling will always eventually admit that it wants to feel great. So let it! You're good enough to withstand the passing disappointments and pain that afflict life on this planet—but trying to protect yourself by believing that you don't embody greatness is overkill.

OCTOBER 14

This may come as a surprise to you, but failure is an illusion. No one ever fails at anything. Everything you do produces a result. If you're trying to learn how to catch a football and someone throws it to you and you drop it, you haven't failed. You simply produced a result. The real question is what you do with the results that you produce. Do you leave, and moan about being a football failure, or do you say, "Throw it again," until ultimately you're catching footballs? Failure is a judgment. It's just an opinion. It comes from your fears, which can be eliminated by love. Love for yourself. Love for what you do. Love for others. Love for your planet. When you have love within you, fear cannot survive. Think of the message in this ancient wisdom: "Fear knocked at the door. Love answered and no one was there."

OCTOBER 15

There is a Chinese proverb, "If you're going to pursue revenge, you'd better dig *two* graves." Your resentments will destroy you.

OCTOBER 16

Make a personal commitment to do what you love
and love what you do—today!

OCTOBER 17

I would like to let you in on a sublime secret that I learned from one of my most influential teachers: *You will only come to truly know God when you give up the past and the future in your mind and merge totally into the now, because God is always here now.*

OCTOBER 18

Take the letters that make up the word *listen* and rearrange them so that they spell out *silent*: *listen/silent—listen/silent*—the same in content only arranged to appear different from each other. When you listen, you'll feel the silence. When you're silent, you'll hear at a new level of listening.

OCTOBER 19

Place your thoughts on what it is you'd like to become—an artist, a musician, a computer programmer, a dentist, or whatever. In your thoughts, begin to picture yourself having the skills to do these things. No doubts. Only a knowing. Then begin acting as if these things were already your reality. As an artist, your vision allows you to draw, to visit art museums, to talk with famous artists, and to immerse yourself in the art world. In other words, you begin to *act* as an artist in all aspects of your life. In this way, you're getting out in front of yourself and taking charge of your own destiny at the same time that you're cultivating inspiration.

OCTOBER 20

Declare yourself to be a genius, to be an expert, to be in an atmosphere of abundance, and keep that vision so passionately that you can do nothing but act upon it. As you do, you will send out the attractor energy that will work with you to materialize your actions based upon those stated declarations.

Treat everyone you encounter with the same intention. Celebrate in others their finest qualities. Treat them all in this "as if" manner, and I guarantee you that they will respond accordingly to your highest expectations. It's all up to you. Whether you think this is possible or impossible, either way you'll be right. And you'll see the rightness of your thoughts manifesting everywhere you go.

OCTOBER 21

I find it helpful to think of my mind as a pond. The surface of the pond is similar to my mental chatter. On the surface are the disturbances. Here there are storms, debris, freezing, and thawing. Beneath the pond surface, there is relative stillness. Here it is quiet and peaceful. If, as has been said, it's true that we have approximately 60,000 separate, often disconnected thoughts during the day, then our mind is like a pond that's full of whitecaps from a choppy breeze. But beneath that surface chatter is the gap where we can know God and gain the unlimited power of reconnecting to our Source.

OCTOBER 22

I am what I do.
I am what I have.
I am separate from God.
I am what others think of me.
I am separate from everyone else.
I am separate from what is missing in my life.

Sometime during our life, we identified ourselves as variations of these six beliefs. Our physical body became the means for identifying ourselves as distinct from others. Possessions, achievements, and reputation became our calling cards. Things we believed were missing became goals. This aspect of ourselves is what I am calling *ego*. We need to tame the ego so that we can regain our all-encompassing Source of power.

OCTOBER 23

We all originate from the same Source of Divine love. As we grow and mature, we are all given free choice to stay connected to this Source, or to edge God out and live by the demands and inclinations of our false self—the ego.

OCTOBER 24

Perhaps the most elusive space for human beings to enter is the gap between our thoughts. Usually we stay on one thought until another one takes over, leaving very little unused space. The spaces between our thoughts are brief, and seldom does anyone wonder what it would be like to have fewer thoughts, or what we'd find in the void between them. But the paradox is obvious. Thinking about what it would be like to be in the gap between our thoughts . . . is just another thought. Rather than expanding that space between, we move on to more thoughts. So why should we concern ourselves with entering the elusive gap? Because everything emerges from the void.

OCTOBER 25

The 31st verse of the Tao Te Ching unequivocally states that implements of violence serve evil. Lao-tzu clearly knew that weapons designed to kill are tools of futility and should be avoided if you choose to live according to the principles of the Tao. The Tao is about life; weapons are about death. The Tao is a creative force; weapons are about destruction.

There's no victory in any activity where killing takes place. Why? Because all people, regardless of their geographic location or belief system, are connected to each other by their originating spirit. We all come from, retain, and return to the Tao. When we destroy each other, we're destroying our opportunity to allow the Tao to *inform* us, to flow freely in and through the form we're in.

OCTOBER 26

There are many opportunities to access silence. I try to meditate each time I stop at a red light. With the car stopped and my body inactive, frequently the only things still moving are the thoughts in my mind. I use those two minutes or so at the stoplight to bring my mind into harmony with my inert car and body. I get a wonderful bonus of silence. I probably stop at a red light 20 or 30 times a day, creating 40 minutes to an hour of silence. And there's always someone behind me to let me know that my time is up by breaking the silence with a honking horn!

OCTOBER 27

You practice forgiveness for two reasons: (1) to let others know that you no longer wish to be in a state of hostility with that person, and (2) to free yourself from the self-defeating energy of resentment. Resentment is like venom that continues to pour through your system, doing its poisonous damage long after you've been bitten by the snake. It's not the bite that kills you; it's the venom. You can remove venom by making a decision to let go of resentments. Send love in some form to those you feel have wronged you and notice how much better you feel, how much more peace you have. It was one act of profound forgiveness toward my own father, whom I never saw or talked to, that turned my life around from one of ordinary awareness to one of higher consciousness, achievement, and success beyond anything I had ever dared to imagine.

OCTOBER 28

There is no place that God is not. Remind yourself of this every day. It has been said that God sleeps in the minerals, rests in the vegetables, walks in the animals, and thinks in us. Think of God as a presence rather than a person—a presence that allows a seed to sprout, that moves the stars across the sky, and that simultaneously moves a thought across your mind; a presence that grows the grass and grows your fingernails . . . all at the same time. This presence is everywhere; therefore, it must also be in *you*!

OCTOBER 29

Become "a knower of the truth," as Lao-tzu advises, by forgetting the locks, chains, maps, and plans. Travel without leaving a trace, trust in the goodness that is the root of all, and rather than curse the darkness that seems so rampant, reach out with that inner light and let it shine on those who aren't seeing their own legacy in the Tao.

❖

OCTOBER 30

There have been many difficult situations I've been faced with that appeared to be the exact opposite of my manifestation efforts. Yet I've come to trust that it's always for the best. What once seemed calamitous now is seen as a Divine blessing. Your job is not to say *how* or *when*, but to say *yes*. After *yes*, become the observer and give thanks for everything. Every time I pick up a coin on the street, I view it as a symbol of the abundance that God sends into my life, and I feel gratitude. I always say, "Thank You, God, for everything." Never do I ask, "Why only a penny?"

OCTOBER 31

Everything you're currently against blocks you from abundance.

NOVEMBER 1

Stop looking for your purpose. Be it!

NOVEMBER 2

To activate the creative forces that lie dormant in your life, you must go to the unseen world, the world beyond your form. Here is where what doesn't exist for you in your world of form will be created. You might think of it in this way: In form, you receive *in-form*ation. When you move to spirit, you receive *in-spir*ation. It is this world of inspiration that will guide you to access anything that you would like to have in your life.

NOVEMBER 3

Everything that you wish to manifest emerges from Spirit, from the silence. You don't use your ego to manifest. In fact, ego can inhibit the creative process. For this reason, I urge you not to divulge your private insights, what you intend to create. . . . When you talk about your emerging manifesting ideas and relate your insights to others, you often feel the need to explain and defend them. What happens is that ego has entered. Once the ego is present, the manifesting stops.

NOVEMBER 4

I once spent an afternoon swimming with the dolphins in the Mexican Riviera. I'd never done such a thing in all of my life. But rather than telling myself that I couldn't undertake such an outing because *it's never happened before*, I reversed the logic and instead thought, *Since I've never done this before, I want to add this to my repertoire and have this unique experience right now.* And it was sensational!

Adopt this kind of thinking regarding everything you've "never done" before. Open up to vistas that bring you to a new way of being where you create wealth, health, and happiness in the present moment.

❖

NOVEMBER 5

Become a person who refuses to be offended by any one, any thing, or any set of circumstances. If something takes place and you disapprove, by all means state what you feel from your heart; and if possible, work to eliminate it and then let it go. Most people operate from the ego and really need to be right. So, when you encounter someone saying things that you find inappropriate, or when you know they're wrong, wrong, wrong, forget your need to be right and instead say, "You're right about that!" Those words will end potential conflict and free you from being offended. Your desire is to be peaceful—not to be right, hurt, angry, or resentful. If you have enough faith in your own beliefs, you'll find that it's impossible to be offended by the beliefs and conduct of others.

NOVEMBER 6

Anonymously perform acts of kindness, expecting nothing in return, not even a thank-you. The universal all-creating Spirit responds to acts of kindness by asking: *How may I be kind to you?*

NOVEMBER 7

I think of the word *inspiration* as meaning "being in-Spirit." When we're in-Spirit, we're inspired . . . and when we're inspired, it's because we're back in-Spirit, fully awake to Spirit within us. Being inspired is an experience of joy: We feel completely connected to our Source and totally on purpose; our creative juices flow, and we bring exceptionally high energy to our daily life. We're not judging others or ourselves—we're uncritical and unbothered by behaviors or attitudes that in uninspired moments are frustrating. Our heart sings in appreciation for every breath, and we're tolerant, joyful, and loving.

NOVEMBER 8

Believe in synchronicity. Don't be surprised when someone you've been thinking about calls out of the blue, when the perfect book arrives unexpectedly in the mail, or when the money to finance a project mysteriously shows up.

NOVEMBER 9

View those tenacious thoughts that just won't go away as intention talking to you, saying, "You signed up to express your unique brilliance, so why do you keep ignoring it?"

NOVEMBER 10

Rather than using language indicating that your desires may not materialize, speak from an inner conviction that communicates your profound and simple knowing that the universal Source supplies everything.

NOVEMBER 11

Begin noticing the frequency of any thoughts
that support the idea of sickness as something to
be expected—and eliminate them from your mind.

NOVEMBER 12

If motivation is grabbing an idea and carrying it through to an acceptable conclusion, then inspiration is the reverse. When we're in the grip of inspiration, an idea has taken hold of us from the invisible reality of Spirit. Something that seems to come from afar, where we allow ourselves to be moved by a force that's more powerful than our ego and all of its illusions, is inspiration. And being in-Spirit is the place where we connect to the invisible reality that ultimately directs us toward our calling. Often we can identify these inspired times by their insistence, and because they seem not to make sense while at the same time they keep appearing in our consciousness.

NOVEMBER 13

Do not give mental energy to what others feel about how you should live your life. This can be a tough assignment at first, but you'll welcome the shift when it happens.

NOVEMBER 14

By banishing doubt and thinking in no-limit ways, you clear a space for the power of intention to flow through you.

NOVEMBER 15

You are a Divine creation of God. You can never be separate from that which created you. If you can think of God as the ocean and yourself as a container, you may find it helpful in moments of doubt, or when you feel lost or alone, to remember that you are a container of God. When you dip your glass into the ocean, what you have is a glass of God. It's not as big or as strong, but it's still God. As long as you refuse to believe otherwise, you won't feel separate from God.

NOVEMBER 16

If you had to search for light, the one thing you'd obviously shun would be the darkness. You'd know for certain that spending your time analyzing dark places and wallowing around blindly in the dark wouldn't be the way to discover and experience the light. Now exchange the words *light* and *dark* in this example for the words *abundance* and *scarcity*—the same logic should now apply. You can't find abundance by analyzing and wallowing around in scarcity consciousness. Yet this is often why a disparity exists between your desire for prosperity and the lack of it in your life.

NOVEMBER 17

Listening exclusively to your left brain will turn you ultimately into a pretender, or even worse, a commuter—getting up every morning going with the crowd, doing that job that brings in the money and pays the bills; and getting up the next morning and doing it all over again, as a well-known song implies. Meanwhile, the music inside of you fades almost to a point of being inaudible. But your constant invisible companion always hears the music and continues tapping you on your shoulder. The attempts to get your attention may take the form of an ulcer, or a fire to burn up your resistance, or being fired from a stifling job, or being brought to your knees with an accident. Usually these accidents, illnesses, and forms of bad luck finally get your attention. But not always. Some people end up like Tolstoy's character Ivan Ilyich, who anguished on his deathbed, "What if my whole life has been wrong?" A fearsome scene, I must say.

❖

NOVEMBER 18

Feel the surge of the life force that allows you to think, sleep, move about, digest, and even meditate. The power of intention responds to your appreciation of it.

NOVEMBER 19

Silence is the one experience you can have that's indivisible. You cut silence in half, and all you get is more silence. There's only one silence. Therefore, silence is your one way to experience the oneness and the indivisibility of God. This is why you want to meditate. This is how you *know God* rather than having to settle for *knowing about God*.

NOVEMBER 20

Persistently viewing others as dishonest, lazy, sin-
ful, and ignorant can be a way of compensating for
something you fear.

NOVEMBER 21

You might fear being successful. You may have been conditioned to believe you're inadequate or limited. The only way to challenge these absurdities is to go toward what you know you're here for and let success chase after you, as it most assuredly will.

NOVEMBER 22

We must make the effort to find our way to that peaceful nothingness while we're still in our body. We can empty our pockets or purses, but we especially need to empty our *mind* and relish the joy of living in our physical world while simultaneously experiencing the bliss of nothingness. This is our origin, just as it is assuredly our ultimate destination as well.

NOVEMBER 23

Quietly retreat from loud, bellicose, opinionated people. Send them a silent blessing and then unobtrusively move along.

NOVEMBER 24

The mind is a powerful tool in creating health. It tells your body to produce the drugs it needs to keep you healthy. Give someone a sugar pill and convince them that it's an anti-arthritic drug, and that person's body will react to the placebo with the increased production of anti-arthritic energies.

Your mind also creates Divine relationships, abundance, harmony in business—and even parking places! If your thoughts are focused on what you want to attract in your life, and you maintain that thought with the passion of an absolute intention, you'll eventually act upon that intention, because the ancestor to every single action is a thought.

NOVEMBER 25

By being big enough to make amends with your so-called enemies, you'll respect yourself much more than prior to your acts of forgiveness.

NOVEMBER 26

In all of your relationships, if you can love someone enough to allow them to be exactly what they choose to be—without any expectations or attachments from you—you'll know true peace in your lifetime. True love means you love a person for what they *are*, not for what you think they *should* be. This is an open mind—*and* an absence of attachment.

NOVEMBER 27

Choose to see death as simply removing a garment or moving from one room into another—it's merely a transition.

❖

NOVEMBER 28

Always find something to appreciate, whether it's the beauty of a starry night, a frog on a lily pad, a laughing child, or the natural radiance and splendor of the aged.

NOVEMBER 29

One of the most effective means for transcending *ordinary* and moving into the realm of the *extraordinary* is saying *yes* more frequently and eliminating *no* almost completely. It's basically *saying yes to life*.

NOVEMBER 30

You cannot remedy anything by condemning it. You only add to the destructive energy that's already permeating the atmosphere of your life.

DECEMBER 1

Once you've accepted your power to heal yourself and optimize your health, you become someone who's capable of healing others as well.

DECEMBER 2

It's really the space between the notes that makes the music you enjoy so much. Without the spaces, all you would have is one continuous noisy note. Everything that's created comes out of silence. Your thoughts emerge from the nothingness of silence. Your words come out of this void. Your very essence emerged from emptiness. Those who will supersede us are waiting in the vast void. All creativity requires some stillness. Your sense of inner peace depends on spending some of your life energy in silence to recharge your battery, remove tension and anxiety, reacquaint you with the joy of knowing God, and feel closer to all of humanity. Silence reduces fatigue and allows you to experience your own creative juices.

DECEMBER 3

It has been said that it's the space between the bars that holds the tiger. And it's the silence between the notes that makes the music. It is out of the silence, or "the gap," or that space between our thoughts, that everything is created—including our own bliss.

DECEMBER 4

Immerse yourself in movies, television shows, plays, and recordings tendered by individuals and organizations that reflect a rapport with Spirit. Simply listening to lectures by great spiritual teachers can increase your daily inspiration level. Also, notice how you feel during explosion and chase scenes in movies that lead to an inevitable overexposure to violence, hatred, and killing. Check yourself in these moments: Do you feel closer to Spirit or further and further removed from It? Use your own intuition to remind yourself when it's time to change the channel or leave the movie theater.

DECEMBER 5

When you become immobilized by what anybody else thinks of you, what you're saying is: "Your opinion of me is more important than my own opinion of myself."

DECEMBER 6

If we ignore inspiration's powerful attraction, the result is personal discomfort or a sense of disconnection from ourselves. For any number of reasons, we might be resistant when we feel called to create, perform, visit a foreign place, meet someone, express ourselves, help another, or be a part of a cause. Inspiration is a calling to proceed even though we're unsure of goals or achievements—it may even insist that we go in the direction of uncharted territory.

DECEMBER 7

I once had a conversation with a neurosurgeon who was disputing the presence of this invisible world by saying that he'd cut into thousands of bodies and had never seen a soul. I remember his awkward look when I asked him if he'd ever seen a thought while he was poking around inside a brain.

DECEMBER 8

Did you ever notice how difficult it is to argue with someone who's not obsessed with being right?

DECEMBER 9

Make a concerted effort to allow the natural healing and well-being capacity of your body to play itself out. Refuse to focus on what's wrong in your body and in your life; rather, shift your thoughts to those that allow you to stay in harmony with your Source energy. For example, rather than saying, "I feel sick," say, "I want to feel good, so I'll allow my natural connection to well-being to take over right now." Your reformed self-talk invites the flow of inspiration.

DECEMBER 10

Heaven should not be thought of as a place you'll ultimately arrive at once you leave this earthly existence. Rather, it seems to me that you'd want to experience Heaven right here on Earth.

DECEMBER 11

If you slip, it doesn't mean that you're less valuable. It simply means you have something to learn from slipping.

DECEMBER 12

The opposite of courage is not so much fear as it is conformity.

DECEMBER 13

I was frequently told as a young boy, and even as a college student, that I didn't possess the necessary talent to be a writer or public speaker. It wasn't until I decided to follow my own inner pictures that my talents began to be heard. Why? Because the more I pursued my life from the balance point of what felt right for me, the more practice I gained, and the more the universe and I were aligned. In that alignment I attracted and recognized all of the opportunities and guidance available to me. Had I listened to those who professed to know better concerning my talents, I would have attracted precisely what I was believing: an absence of ability.

DECEMBER 14

If you find yourself being treated in a way you resent or that turns you into a victim, ask yourself this question: "What have I done to teach this person that this behavior is something I'm willing to tolerate?"

DECEMBER 15

You have the ability to enter higher regions so as to consciously fulfill your highest desires here, now, for the greater benefit of all. This is akin to doing a somersault and landing in a new reality—a reality in which all things are possible, a reality where you no longer identify yourself with all of those cultural memes and mind viruses that were programmed into you as a young person, preparing you for an ordinary life.

DECEMBER 16

Even if you don't know what you should be doing or what your mission is, you need to practice creating that vision anyway.

DECEMBER 17

For a long time we were required to hate Russians, then Iranians; we could love the Iraqis, but only for a short time. Then we reversed those on the hate list: We were obliged to hate the formerly loved Iraqis, and it was okay to love the Iranians we were told to hate only 10 years before. Then came the Taliban, and even more obscure categories such as terrorists whom we used to be required to love, and insurgents, whoever they are now, became mandatory targets of our hate.

On and on goes this litany of hate! The faces change, but the message remains: We're told whom to hate, never for a moment recognizing that the enemy we're supposed to hate isn't a nationality—*the enemy is hatred itself!*

DECEMBER 18

A television interviewer once asked me if I ever felt guilty about making so much from my writings and recordings. I responded, much to her surprise, "I would feel guilty, except that it's not my fault." When she asked what I meant, I explained that money has always come to me because I've always felt within me that I *am* money. I attract prosperity because I feel entitled to it; in fact, I feel that it's actually a definition of me. . . .

When I was a little kid, I saw that collecting soda-pop bottles would bring in pennies and that pennies became dollars. I saw that helping ladies with their groceries, shoveling their snow, or emptying their ashes from the coal furnaces were acts of prosperity. And today, I'm still collecting pop bottles, shoveling snow, and carrying out ashes on a much larger scale. Prosperity continues to chase after me because I'm still in total harmony with my originating Spirit, which is abundance and prosperity.

DECEMBER 19

Anything that keeps you from growing is never worth defending.

DECEMBER 20

Attempting to do something, even if it doesn't succeed, is inspiring because we don't tend to regret what we do; we regret what we *didn't* do.

DECEMBER 21

Acquaint yourself with the subconscious mind. Your subconscious mind acts on what you program into it, so that it becomes your automatic mind acting habitually. Decide on a habit that you would like to be automatic—being generous, for example. Tell yourself, *I am a generous person.* Give something away in a spirit of generosity, even if it's only a small coin or a word of encouragement. The more thoughts and actions you practice around your new *I am*, the more the subconscious mind will react in kind until eventually it will act in generous ways out of a new habit that you've created. You have the power to impress upon the subconscious mind any *I am* of your choosing.

DECEMBER 22

If you play the game of life, know that you'll have plenty of wins and losses, regardless of your talent level.

DECEMBER 23

The secret to rebalancing life is not necessarily to change your behavior as much as it is to realign yourself and *create a culture that supersedes the cycles of battle and retreat*. Whenever we use force to resolve our disputes, we instantly create a counterforce. This is largely responsible for the never-ending cycles of war that have defined human history. Force, counterforce, more force, and the battles go on, generation after generation.

This is true within you as well: A thought of hate creates a thought of revenge, and then more hateful thoughts in response. And the real problem is that these thoughts of hatred and revenge begin to define your existence. Your desire to live peacefully is a spiritually balanced desire. In order to materialize your desire, you must extend thoughts that match the energy of that desire. Thoughts of hate will not blossom into your desired peacefulness. *You attract more and more of that which you desire to eradicate.*

DECEMBER 24

Remember this simple truth: *The answer to how is yes*. You may never know exactly how you're going to accomplish the feeling of inspiration, but by saying *yes!* to life and all that calls you, the how will take care of itself.

DECEMBER 25

Just as we're all students throughout life, we're all teachers. In fact, we learn best by offering what we desire for ourselves to as many individuals as we can, as frequently as we can. If I instruct enough people for a long enough period of time, I'll teach what *I* most want to learn.

DECEMBER 26

The greatest gift you were ever given was the gift of your imagination. Within your magical inner realm is the capacity to have all of your wishes fulfilled. Here in your imagination lies the greatest power you will ever know. It is your domain for creating the life that you desire, and the best part of it is that you are the monarch with all of the inherent powers to rule your world as you desire.

DECEMBER 27

Follow your right brain, listening to how you feel, and play your own unique brand of music. You won't have to fear anything or anyone, and you'll never experience that terror of lying on your deathbed someday, saying, "What if my whole life has been wrong?" Your invisible companion on your right shoulder will prod you each and every time you're moving away from your purpose. It makes you aware of your music. So listen— and don't die with that music still in you.

DECEMBER 28

I anticipate a planet at peace—along with health, abundance, and love in my life and in the lives of all others—and I know that it's moving in this direction. I know that for every act of apparent evil, there are a million acts of kindness. That's where I place my attention, and that's what I choose to give away. . . . I watch the mynah birds singing every morning, and I know they're not doing it because they have the answers to all of life's problems—they have a song inside of them that they obviously feel compelled to let come out. I too have a song to sing, and by staying in-Spirit I'm able to sing it all day, every day.

I know that the answer to "What should I be doing?" is to see the word *yes* on my inner screen: "Yes, I am listening"; "Yes, I am paying attention"; and most important, "Yes, I am willing."

DECEMBER 29

You are a uniquely Divine creation. You share the same life force that was in Moses, Jesus, Buddha, Mother Teresa, Mohammed, Saint Francis, or any Divine being you can name. There is only one life force, one Divine power. When it manifests as doubt, fear, hate, or even evil, it's still the one power, but it's moving away from God in ego consciousness. When it manifests as faith, joy, forgiveness, hope, light, and love, it's the same force—either moving toward God or in harmony with God consciousness.

DECEMBER 30

Dedicate your life to something that reflects an awareness of your Divinity. You are greatness personified, a resident genius, and a creative master—regardless of anyone's opinion. Make a silent dedication to encourage and express your Divine nature.

DECEMBER 31

In essence, I'm urging you to stop taking your life so personally. You can end any and all suffering by reminding yourself that nothing in the universe is personal. Of course you've been taught to take life very personally, but this is an illusion. Tame your ego, and absolutely free yourself from ever taking anything personally.

ABOUT THE AUTHOR

Affectionately called the "father of motivation" by his fans, **Dr. Wayne W. Dyer** was an internationally renowned author, speaker, and pioneer in the field of self-development. Over the four decades of his career, he wrote more than 40 books (21 of which became *New York Times* bestsellers), created numerous audio programs and videos, and appeared on thousands of television and radio shows. His books *Manifest Your Destiny, Wisdom of the Ages, There's a Spiritual Solution to Every Problem,* and the *New York Times* bestsellers *10 Secrets for Success and Inner Peace, The Power of Intention, Inspiration, Change Your Thoughts—Change Your Life, Excuses Begone!, Wishes Fulfilled,* and *I Can See Clearly Now* were all featured as National Public Television specials.

Wayne held a doctorate in educational counseling from Wayne State University, had been an associate professor at St. John's University in New York, and honored a lifetime commitment to learning and finding the Higher Self. In 2015, he left his body, returning to Infinite Source to embark on his next adventure.

Website: www.DrWayneDyer.com

Hay House Titles of Related Interest

YOU CAN HEAL YOUR LIFE, the movie,
starring Louise Hay & Friends
(available as a 1-DVD program, an expanded 2-DVD set,
and an online streaming video)
Learn more at www.hayhouse.com/louise-movie

THE SHIFT, the movie,
starring Dr. Wayne W. Dyer
(available as a 1-DVD program, an expanded 2-DVD set,
and an online streaming video)
Learn more at www.hayhouse.com/the-shift-movie

◆◆

FALLING UP: My Wild Ride from Victim to Kick-Ass Victor,
by Dana Liesegang, with Natasha Stoynoff

THE GIFT OF FIRE: How I Made Adversity Work for Me,
by Dan Caro

*LEFT TO TELL: Discovering God Amidst the
Rwandan Holocaust,* by Immaculée Ilibagiza

*MAKING LIFE EASY: How the Divine Inside Can Heal Your
Body and Your Life,* by Christiane Northrup, M.D.

*WHAT IF THIS IS HEAVEN?: How Our Cultural Myths Prevent
Us from Experiencing Heaven on Earth,*
by Anita Moorjani

All of the above are available at your local bookstore,
or may be ordered by contacting Hay House (see next page).

◆◆

We hope you enjoyed this Hay House book. If you'd like to receive our online catalog featuring additional information on Hay House books and products, or if you'd like to find out more about the Hay Foundation, please contact:

Hay House, Inc., P.O. Box 5100, Carlsbad, CA 92018-5100
(760) 431-7695 or (800) 654-5126
(760) 431-6948 (fax) or (800) 650-5115 (fax)
www.hayhouse.com® • www.hayfoundation.org

———

Published in Australia by:
Hay House Australia Pty. Ltd., 18/36 Ralph St., Alexandria NSW 2015
Phone: 612-9669-4299 • *Fax:* 612-9669-4144
www.hayhouse.com.au

Published in the United Kingdom by:
Hay House UK Ltd, The Sixth Floor, Watson House,
54 Baker Street, London W1U 7BU
Phone: +44 (0)20 3927 7290 • *Fax:* +44 (0)20 3927 7291
www.hayhouse.co.uk

Published in India by:
Hay House Publishers India, Muskaan Complex, Plot No. 3, B-2,
Vasant Kunj, New Delhi 110 070
Phone: 91-11-4176-1620 • *Fax:* 91-11-4176-1630
www.hayhouse.co.in

———

Access New Knowledge.
Anytime. Anywhere.

Learn and evolve at your own pace
with the world's leading experts.

www.hayhouseU.com